Christ, the Cross and the Concrete Jungle

John Caldwell

EP BOOKS

1st Floor Venture House, 6 Silver Court, Watchmead, Welwyn Garden City, UK, AL7 1TS

web: http://www.epbooks.org

e-mail: sales@epbooks.org

EP Books are distributed in the USA by:
JPL Distribution
3741 Linden Avenue Southeast
Grand Rapids, MI 49548
E-mail: orders@jpldistribution.com
Tel: 877.683.6935

British Library Cataloguing in Publication Data available

ISBN 978–1–78397–075–9

Printed by Bell and Bain Ltd, Glasgow

Contents

Dedication

To Steven (Morry), Martin, Anton, James, Louise Anne, Rachael, Gillian and all the gang from Paisley YMCA.

Dictionary of Local Dialect

Ah: I.

Awrite: Literally means 'Alright' and is a way of saying 'Okay'.

Aye: Yes.

Close: Stairwell of a tenement building.

Crash/Crashed: To spend the night or to sleep, e.g., to crash (sleep) on the couch. Or, to crash at a friend's house.

Dae: Do.

Dodgy: Illegal, untrustworthy.

Fag/fags: Cigarette/cigarettes.

Guid: Good.

How: Why, e.g., 'How no?' means 'Why not?'

Naw: No.

No: Not.

Old-Firm: A collective term for two Glasgow based rival Scottish football teams: Celtic Football Club and Rangers Football Club. (An 'old-firm top' is a Celtic or Rangers shirt.)

Pop: Go (briefly), e.g., to pop (go) into a shop.

Popped: Went (briefly). e.g. I popped (went) into the shop.

Proddy: Protestant (as in a person connected to the Protestant church as opposed to the Roman Catholic church.)

Tablet: Confectionery.

Tae: To.

Trainers: Footwear ('Sneakers' in USA).

Trakkie: Literally, Tracksuit (Sportswear).

Wasted: Drunk.

Weans: Children.

Wee: Small

Whit: What.

Wir: Were

Wrecked: Drunk.

Ye: You.

Yer: Your.

Acknowledgements

I am forever indebted to Laura and Allana for helping to prepare the manuscript for publication and also for constant feedback throughout the project. Additional thanks is due to Laura for her patience and understanding as I have devoted many hours to this project. People often ask me, how do I manage to work full time, prepare sermons, cover vacant churches and write? My response is always the same: I have an excellent wife who is an incredible support! Thanks also to Graham Hind and the directors at Evangelical Press for seeing the potential in this book. I'm also incredibly grateful to my editor Trudy, whose attention to detail has helped to make *Christ, the Cross and the Concrete Jungle* a better book. The final word of thanks belongs to God the Father of my Lord Jesus Christ for His amazing grace which 'saved a wretch like me'. I thank God that He has not only saved me, but He has also given me the privilege of making known to others the saving work of Calvary. To God be the glory.

.

1

Glimpses of Chaos

SIXTEEN years ago, I awoke in a cell in Giffnock Police Station. The police officer had just clattered the cell door and shouted through the gap that it was time for me to be released. I was hungover, disorientated, cold, choking for a fag, and could only vaguely remember why I happened to be in a cell. I was eighteen years old, and this was the first time I'd been arrested.

I was accompanied to the front desk by the police officer, given my trainers back and informed that I would be given a date for court. I simply responded by asking, 'What did I do?'

'You took a baseball bat to several car windscreens,' replied the officer. The truth was, I was so drunk the night before that I could barely remember any of it.

Here I was being released from the police station with no money, fags or any way of getting back to Barrhead. Actually, I had no idea where Giffnock was. I asked the desk sergeant how I was to get home, to which he bluntly replied, 'Walk.' After getting some directions, I made my way to a phone box; I was supposed to be working with my godfather that morning. I called the operator, reversed the charges and asked the guys to pick me up in the work van.

As I waited at a bus stop for them to arrive, I tried to piece together the jumbled collection of hazy memories from the previous night. I remembered meeting up with an old schoolmate and drinking some cans of lager. We then bought cider and later some vodka. By the end of the evening we were wasted. As we were chatting, I recalled a recent incident in which I'd been attacked by a guy from one of the other schemes. I was outside a shop with a mate, we were about to buy a carry out, and the guy came towards me wielding nunchakas.

It was only seconds into the pursuit when I felt the thud of the nunchakas on my right shoulder. I continued running, and my pursuer turned back. The guy was after me because I owed him money and he was fed up waiting for it. After discussing this with my mate, he informed me that the fellow had moved into a house on a street nearby. Fuelled by alcohol, we headed to my Mum's house for a baseball bat in order to go and see if we could find him.

The rest of the details are lost to me. From what I've been told, we tried several houses to no avail. Somewhere along the line I got myself into a bit of frenzy and began to smack lamp posts, fences and car windscreens with the baseball bat. I think I smashed approximately half a dozen car windscreens that night. As I was too drunk to run very far, the police had no problem in catching me.

I share this story not to portray myself as some sort of hard man. I wasn't. Neither do I share it in order to glorify the incident. There is no glory in it; it was a senseless act of vandalism. I share it in order to give a glimpse of the level of chaos my life had spiralled into by the time I was eighteen years old.

BEGINNINGS

My early childhood was quite normal and happy. I grew up in the small town of Johnstone in Renfrewshire with my Mum and Stepdad. A few years later, my younger sister came along, and a few years after that, my younger brother. There were grandparents on both sides of the family, both parents worked and both grandparents would babysit. Both sides of the family were Roman Catholic, so we also went to church (chapel) regularly on Sundays. All in all, things were happy and normal.

Although I was growing up with a stepdad, I am not sure I had a real awareness of this fact. I do remember being at my Mum and Stepdad's wedding at the age of four, but I have no recollection of my biological dad whatsoever. My Mum's first marriage ended when I was still a baby. My Mum remarried, and family life was reasonably stable.

Trouble

However, trouble was to hit the Caldwell home in the early nineties. The difficulty was in the form of an extra-marital affair, followed by separation and divorce. I was about ten years old, my sister was five and my brother was three when we learned that 'Dad was leaving because he was seeing another woman'. Looking back, I realise that I did not really understand what was happening, but I knew it was bad. The sense of grief was tangible; pressure and stress filled the very atmosphere of the home.

Mum was devastated by the circumstances; in order to deal with the pain, she immersed herself in music. I still remember the many nights where the record player would be playing constantly and the songs of Paul Simon and REO Speedwagon could be heard in every room in the house.

3

A short while after the separation, my Mum began a relationship with a guy called Mick who was not from our area. He would often come round in the evenings and they would have a drink. Initially this was quite novel; he seemed quite witty and outgoing. He also did not seem as strict as the other adults. He would swear a lot, tell dirty jokes and boast about various exploits of violence.

The violence did not remain in his stories though. One night Mick arrived at the house having been out drinking, to find my Stepdad at the house. An argument broke out which led to a fight and my stepdad being seriously injured. We fled in a taxi to Mick's sister's home in Barrhead. We stayed there for the weekend and then returned to Johnstone once the dust had settled. Upon returning to Johnstone, we quickly discovered that a feud was now underway. There were several people with an axe to grind with both Mick and my Mum. Plans were soon put in place to move from Johnstone to Barrhead.

NO BOUNDARIES

With my Stepdad's affair and the separation that followed, along with Mick's arrival, it seemed that the boundaries had now shifted. In actual fact, where there once had been boundaries there were now none. While previously there would sometimes be drinking in our home at the weekend, this was now a regular occurrence. Mick was constantly telling stories about various crimes that he'd committed as a boy and as a young man. Violence was glorified, alcohol flowed freely and morals were mocked. The Catholic influence, although not a major part of family life, was quickly dissolving.

Mick was always devising schemes to make a bit of cash on the side. One dark winter night I joined him on an excursion along the railway line at the back of our house. It was late. I was about ten years old and most boys my age were finishing their homework and getting ready for bed. While many of my peers were learning maths and English, I was learning the principles of urban economics and enterprise; we were stealing scrap metal.

NEW BEGINNINGS
As a family, we relocated to Barrhead. This was Mick's neck of the woods. Johnstone had too much history and was too close to my Stepdad's family. We applied for a council house and within a short period of time received news that we were being offered one. I was filled with excitement at the thought of a new home, new location and new friends. In my imagination I anticipated that brighter days lay ahead; I could not have been more wrong.

We had been offered a house in a place in Barrhead at that time known as 'the scheme' or sometimes 'the bottom scheme' (due to its geographical location). It was a council estate on the borders of Nitshill and Pollok. It still exists, but the scheme that you would find today is a very different place compared to how it was when we moved there. The old houses have since either been demolished or refurbished, and many of the homes were sold to private land owners. That area in Barrhead is quite respectable now, and the image it once portrayed is all but a distant memory.

THE SCHEME
I remember arriving at the new house for the first time. Any romantic notions that filled my mind were soon dispersed as we approached this dark, towering, four-

in-a-block flat. Our dull grey, unpainted house stood out from the other white-washed flats, at the top of a hill, next to a winding alley. Its high iron rail fencing gave it an even more unwelcoming feel. Every house in that four-in-a-block had windows and doors that were boarded up with metal cladding. It looked like a prison camp. There were many houses in the street with the same metal barriers. I asked my Mum, 'Why are there metal cases on all the windows?'

'It's to keep the animals out,' she sarcastically replied.

The surrounding estate was dark and had a very hostile feel to it. There were several gangs of young people at various sections of the street. Some younger kids were putting stones and bottles through someone's letter box. The woman in the house began to scream at them, but no one seemed to bother. The realisation dawned upon me that our new area was not safe.

I had been warned about the tough nature of the scheme before arriving. Several times a week I would hear the instruction, 'You will have to toughen up when you move to this new area.' Never one for getting into fights, the prospect had not exactly thrilled me. I wasn't exactly sure how I was supposed to 'toughen up', but I quickly got the impression that challenging times lay ahead.

The House

Inside, the new house was not much better. The previous tenants had left the rooms full of junk, which was still to be uplifted by the local council. Excrement had been spread all over the bathroom wall. My introduction to the various local gangs and their members was made easier by the graffiti that decorated all the doors and walls inside the house. The house was freezing; a bitterly cold wind blew through the holes in the metal cladding as we set about the task of cleaning and painting.

By the time we moved to the new area, I was about to start primary seven. The alley at the side of our house led up to the primary school. Behind our house was a huge grass playing area which I soon discovered was the local battleground for gang fights. It was also where stolen cars were disposed of and set alight.

LIFE IN THE SCHEME

The part of Johnstone where we had lived previously was no leafy suburb by any means, but this scheme was a whole new level altogether. I remember one of my first encounters with one of the local guys. He was a couple of years older than me. Our paths crossed as I was making my way to the shop. He was writing his name on the ground with paint. It was a name that I'd seen scrawled over many fences, walls and bus stops.

'Whit's yer name?' he asked, continuing his masterpiece without looking up. 'John,' I replied as I slowed down, almost to a halt.

'Are ye a guid fighter?' he asked in a matter-of-fact sort of way. Quickly searching my thoughts for the right thing to say, 'Aye,' I blurted out.

'Dae ye want tae fight me?' he asked, unperturbed as he continued doodling with the bright orange paint. I paused, thinking that fighting this guy was the last thing I wanted to do. 'Naw,' I said.

'How no?' He stopped what he was doing and looked up at me intently. 'I thought ye said you wir a guid fighter.'

'I don't see the point, I don't even know ye,' I reasoned. Looking puzzled, he shrugged his shoulders and continued marking his territory in bright orange paint. I continued my own journey to the shop for milk.

I mentioned earlier that I was never really one for fighting. It always puzzled me when people wanted to pick fights with me. Perhaps my natural tendency towards pacifism drew more aggressive types towards me like a magnet. Perhaps they could smell fresh meat and easy prey. Either way, I never could understand it. As a youngster I also never considered myself to be very bright. However, looking back, I can see that I was actually quite sharp and had an uncanny ability to get myself out of trouble.

On one occasion, while living in Johnstone, I was playing on my bike in the streets. I would have been in primary five at the time. Two guys, the same age as me, approached me and initiated a conversation. I knew one of them; he was in my class. The other guy went to the Protestant School, and I did not know him so well.

'He wants tae fight ye,' said Tam (the guy I did not know), pointing to Brian (my classmate).

'What for?'

'To see who's the best fighter.'

'Why don't *you* fight him?' I asked as I stood with my bike, wondering how I was going to get out of this one.

'We've already fought,' declared Tam.

'Who won?'

'Ah did,' they replied simultaneously.

A thought quickly flashed through my mind as they began to argue between themselves over who had won the fight.

'Tell ye whit,' I said. 'Why don't ye fight each other to see who wins, and then I'll fight him.'

Amazingly, they both agreed to my suggestion and within seconds both of them were rolling on the ground, knocking lumps out of each other. As soon as the fight was underway, I quickly hopped on my bike and sped down the street, glancing over my shoulder, only to catch both of them looking up with rather puzzled expressions as they held on to each other, clearly wondering what had just happened!

These stories are quite humorous, but the reality is they are nothing compared to the level of social chaos that characterised life in the scheme. Poverty, high divorce rates, unemployment, crime and addiction were widespread factors there.

Looking back, I can see that as a young boy, I was completely unprepared for what would become my new environment. Over the next few years I would be exposed to horrific depths of violence and social dysfunction. Life would become a matter of survival. Eventually, I would begin to embody the very social behaviours I was seeing demonstrated on a daily basis. I would begin to make my own choices, and these choices would lead me on a downward spiral of delinquency, a downward spiral that was going to end either in prison or the grave.

2

Coping with Chaos

SCOTLAND is no stranger to crime and addiction. Stories of senseless evil and tragedy are brought to our awareness on a daily basis. Yet one of the things that marked life in the scheme was its intense depth of darkness. Darkness did not just appear periodically; darkness dwelt in the scheme permanently.

We lived in the bottom scheme for approximately two years. The window into human brokenness was an education in itself. Gangs would meet to fight in the park behind our house. I can still remember the first time I saw two mobs running towards each other with meat cleavers, bricks and bottles.

When I first arrived in the area, a gang of eleven children aged approximately eleven to thirteen broke into the school in broad daylight. As they ran past my garden carrying all sorts of stolen goods, one of them shouted to me,

'D'ya want some paper?' I loved drawing.

'Aye,' I replied, and a huge pack of poster paper was thrown over the fence.

I mentioned earlier that it was a regular occurrence for stolen cars to be abandoned in the park outside our house and set on fire. After the familiar bang of the explosion, a typical scene would follow. The Fire Service would turn up and put out the fire, the police would arrive and take some details then leave and opportunists would appear and strip the car of any redeemable parts!

On another occasion, a crowd of young people began to kick in the school windows in broad daylight. I remember being amazed by their lack of fear of getting caught. On a more serious note, one morning, as I was walking to school along with the other children, we noticed that the top end of the alley had been cordoned off with police tape. A body had been found that morning. It was later reported that a local guy had been shot and stabbed to death, wrapped in a carpet and set on fire.

I also remember the first time I encountered something of the despair that was being experienced by people in the community. A woman, several doors down the street, had attempted to commit suicide by cutting her throat. The neighbours were in a panic trying to save her—fortunately, they managed to help her in time.

Substance abuse was rife in the scheme. A young woman who was well known to everyone would often be seen walking through the scheme 'buzzing' a bag of glue. She was a very chatty person. I always remember her being one of the more friendly faces in the area. One night I was out walking my dog, and she said, 'Mate, it's no a German Shepherd ye need in this place, it's a lion!' She was always full of banter, but looking back, I can see she was in desperate need. Sadly, a few years later she was found dead in the street.

HOME LIFE
Life in the home became a reflection of life in the scheme. There was a lot of heavy drinking, and I always had a sense

of insecurity regarding how the events of an evening would unfold. Mick was given to drinking huge amounts of alcohol, and it was not unusual to experience the four seasons in one night. At times the mood in the home would be jovial; at other times it would be aggressive and hostile. Fights would break out between him and my Mum, and at times became physical. There were many nights I had to run from the house to the nearest phone box (half a mile away) to call the police because of the violence that was taking place. For the next several years our home life would become marked by alcoholism and domestic abuse. Looking back, I realise that my Mum was caught in the trap of an abusive relationship and that she did the best that she could in the circumstances.

Mick's behaviour became increasingly aggressive and unstable. At times he would take his anger out on me and my siblings; at other times my Mum would bear the brunt. On a few occasions Mick tried to take his own life. I remember, one night, having to run to the public pay phone in order to call an ambulance because he had taken an overdose of prescription drugs as well as excessive amounts of alcohol.

At times Mick would get into fights with other people. One night he forced his way into his ex-brother-in-law's house and attacked him. This incident led to Mick being sentenced to several months in jail. The months that Mick was in jail were the calmest and most stable time that I can remember experiencing in those days.

In the midst of the chaos I can remember living with a sense of apprehension and anxiety. Any night that my folks were drinking, I would go to bed worrying that things would get violent. I remember as a youngster making a promise to myself that I would never drink alcohol or go to pubs. I wanted to avoid the madness that seemed to accompany it.

After two years in the scheme, we moved to another part of town. A regeneration project was in place. Houses in the scheme were to be demolished and the people were being relocated from the scheme to another part of town. The new council estate had all the same social problems as the bottom scheme, but they did not seem to be as obvious. During a court case, which involved charges relating to firearms and drug dealing, the area we moved to was described by a court official as 'an area that was known for the use of drugs.' This is an accurate description of that part of Barrhead. In the mid-nineties, there were at least four drug dealers operating from three streets which ran parallel to each other. In those days, heroin had not really made its way into Barrhead; it was mostly 'hash', 'speed', 'LSD' and 'jellies'. However, in just a few years, heroin would make its way in. While the regeneration of the geographical location of the bottom scheme was a success, the authorities just shifted the social problems to another part of town.

SURVIVAL

Growing up in my new area became a matter of survival. Very often a trip to the shop was more like running the gauntlet than going for groceries! To go anywhere, school, shops, or friends' homes, I usually had to pass several gangs posted at various parts of the housing scheme. I may as well have carried a target on my back. I was the new face in town, and people wanted to know who I was, where I was from and what I was made of. I was in no way prepared for the level of aggression that I would face regularly. I seem to remember, from the age of twelve to fourteen, getting a 'kicking' on a regular basis. Anytime I had to go anywhere I would often have to make a run for it or plan some alternative route.

Looking back, I realise that survival in the schemes is not just about being a good fighter or having a carefree attitude. Survival is very much tied in with who you are connected to or, more specifically, who you are related to. Very often, when you are new to a place, before someone will pick a fight with you, he will try to find out who you are and who your local relatives are. While we had moved to the area and my Mum was seeing a local guy, I had no family surname that was associated with anyone from the area. This made me easy prey. Being well connected is half the battle to surviving in the scheme.

Between the constant drinking and violence that went on in our home and the regular conflict with locals who wanted to make a name for themselves, I began to experience a wide range of emotions which became part of daily life. Fear and anxiety were constant companions; anger and frustration also simmered deep within. At times a desire to become more aggressive and streetwise would take hold of me.

SCHOOL DAYS

As a youngster, adults would often say to me, usually when they were drunk, 'school days are the best days of your life,' and 'stick in at school.' This would often be followed with, 'Don't waste your education, make something of yourself and don't become like me.'

I hated school. I resented the authority of school teachers; I struggled to integrate socially. I had very poor motivation when it came to work. Even in subjects that I enjoyed, my lack of motivation won over any interest that

I had in them. Report cards told the same story year after year: 'could do better'.

In class, rather than get on with the work, I'd much prefer to talk or have a carry on. School became an unyielding battle of wills between me and the classroom teachers. The belt had been abolished by the time I was in school, but punishment exercises were regularly handed in my direction, and I spent much of my time standing outside classrooms. As I hit into my teens, the classic metamorphosis took place, and I began to develop more of an attitude. Rather than getting dragged into fights against my will, I found myself starting fights.

RINGSIDE REDEMPTION

At the age of thirteen I became involved in the local boxing club. At first I went along out of curiosity, but it was not long before I was fully committed.

Boxing gave me a focus that I did not have before. The training quickly paid off, and I soon discovered that I was reasonably good at the sport. The boxing instructors began to prepare some of us for amateur fights. For many of us, the discipline of training for fights helped us stay out of trouble.

I began boxing at the age of thirteen. At that time, many of my peers were starting to spend their evenings in parks drinking cider and smoking. Boxing was too important for me to allow that stuff to hold any form of temptation over me. I was not interested. The boxing club became a haven for me, a place free from the conflicts and pressures of home, school and the streets.

As I began to contend in amateur competitions, my love for boxing increased. I can still remember the rush of adrenaline as the bell rang at the start of each fight.

After fighting in several competitions, my plan was to turn professional as soon as I was old enough. I remember getting to the stage in school where Personal Social Development teachers wanted to know what each pupil intended to do with their life when the time came to leave school; my answer was simple: 'become a professional boxer'. Of course the response from the teacher was just as direct: 'that's not a proper career'. I did not quite see the wisdom of this logic; school wasn't exactly working out whereas boxing seemed to offer some form of hope.

Boxing began to have some other benefits. Every so often, some of the various 'young teams' would turn up at the gym, give it a try for a few weeks and then disappear again. Most of them turned up so that they could spar. The opportunity to practice fighting in the ring had a certain amount of appeal. Many of these guys had reputations as great fighters outside in the streets. Since most of them were smoking, drinking and doing drugs outside of the ring, and due to the fact that they had spent no real time training, when it came to fighting in the ring, they could not compete with the guys who were training on a regular basis. The outcome of this was that I began to gain a bit of respect among some of the local young teams. During the evenings when I was out for a run, I would often pass them without getting any hassle, and friendly acknowledgements would often be exchanged instead of the usual barrage of abuse.

THE WINDS OF CHANGE

The Barrhead boxing club saw many young people come and go. Occasionally guys who had boxed in the past but had drifted away for some reason or other would turn up looking to get back into the game. One of the former boxers who turned up stayed in the same part of town as me. Since we lived near each other, we would end up walking home together after training. The guy was a few years older than me, but he seemed really keen to get back into boxing. He told the guys who were running the club that he was keen to get involved in amateur competitions.

I remember the first night we began walking home together. After getting far enough away from the gym, he opened up his gym bag and brought out a one-litre bottle of cider. He cracked it open and drank it as we walked home. He said, smiling awkwardly,

'I've picked up some bad habits that I need to break if I'm going to start boxing again.'

I remember looking at him enjoying the cider and thinking that he didn't look like he was in a hurry to break this habit!

On another night he ducked in behind a wall and asked me to keep an eye out for the police. He began to produce cigarette papers, cigarettes, a lighter and what looked like a small brown rock.

'Do you know what this is?'

I had a fair idea. It was a lump of cannabis.

He rolled his joint, lit it and we walked home. He began to describe how great it felt and how much it 'chilled you right out'. Not long into our walk, after taking a long puff, he held the joint out towards me.

'Do you want a draw?'

'Naw, yer awrite,' I replied, and we continued walking.

While our home life was chaotic with alcohol addiction and other problems, my folks had zero tolerance when it came to drugs. Mick was old school. He told me that he wouldn't mind if I got drunk, fought or broke into shops, but if I took drugs I'd get the beating of my life. I avoided drugs like the plague, partly out of fear of direct consequences (in the nineties there was a high number of young people dying in night clubs from taking ecstasy tablets), but mostly out of fear of getting a severe beating.

Mick was extremely anti-drugs. I remember one night returning home from being out with my friends and being interrogated regarding my activities. Mick was drunk and for some reason was convinced that I was 'on something'. After intense interrogation, where I denied having taken anything. I ended up getting a severe thrashing anyway! Despite the injustice, such experiences proved to be a good deterrent!

When I returned home after the gym that night, I couldn't get the thought of the joint out of my head. The words 'it chills you right out' kept coming back to me. I determined within myself that the next time I had the chance, I wasn't going to pass it by.

3

The Transition

TURNING fifteen was like approaching a crossroads. School, for the most part, was not going well. The upcoming exams were not looking too promising. Besides, there were more interesting things taking place. Social activities had increased and schoolwork was but an obstacle to be avoided. Even boxing began to fade into the background. Girls were on the radar. Most weekends, and a few week nights, would be spent at the Paisley Ice Skating Rink.

I'd managed to get myself a good-paying paper round; I also made some cash through selling macaroon and tablet bars. Not the most glorious way to make cash, but it brought in a steady flow of money that enabled me to travel into Paisley on a regular basis.

Somewhere along the line, things began to change. At some point I made certain choices that would plunge me headfirst into a lifestyle of extreme hedonism. Eventually my reason for living could be summed up in the phrase, 'Wine, women and song' or the more modern version, 'Sex, drugs and rock and roll'. (Although Rock and Roll was an out-dated genre in those days; in the mid-nineties rave music and Oasis were the in thing).

Looking back, I can see that it was not only my behaviour that had changed; my attitude of heart had changed. I stopped caring about other people, and I even stopped caring about myself. Somehow, I had discovered the self-destruct button.

FREEDOM

Leaving school and getting a job only intensified my lifestyle choice. More money and more freedom led to more partying. Initially, my drinking was on a par with my peers'. In the early days it was just the typical teenage experimentation, someone's parents would go out of town, word would spread about an 'empty' and everyone would turn up with alcohol. However, since I looked a few years older than I actually was by the time I was sixteen I was able to get into a few night clubs and pubs. It was only a matter of time until I transitioned from social drinking to anti-social drinking.

When I first left school, I started a catering course at Reid Kerr College (more commonly known as 'Can't Read and Don't Care'), but this did not last long; for one thing, it didn't pay anything. I applied for a job as a trainee chef through the government's Skill Seekers programme. This meant you were working full time, receiving training, and being paid a fraction of a wage. I kept this job for about six months but was eventually sacked for repeatedly being late, taking days off and turning up unfit for work because of the previous night's drinking session.

I eventually got a job with my godfather who owned a roof tiling and slating company. This paid good money, provided great banter but also led to another level of drinking. Very often after work we would hit the pub. I began to enjoy drinking with the older guys from the work more than I enjoyed drinking with my peers.

CONFLICT AT HOME

Things hadn't changed much at home; if anything, things had got worse. Mum worked hard, often working three jobs at the one time. Most days she would begin one cleaning job at 6:00 am, a second full-time job at 8:00 am, finish at 5:00 pm to then go to another two-hour cleaning job at 5:30 pm. Mick would stay at home, watch TV and occasionally get a short-term job.

The drinking and fighting remained a constant aspect of home life. Almost every night Mick would walk across the road to the shop. A bottle of vodka and a couple of beers would be the standard diet three nights a week; on Friday and Saturday it would be a litre of vodka and half a dozen beers. Most of the fights would break out at the weekends.

I made a point of taking a drive to my old street the day I passed my driving test. I popped into the shop and got talking to the older shopkeeper's son. I mentioned I used to live across the road. The guy remembered me. 'That's right,' he said. 'Your old man used to buy a bottle of vodka every night!' Clearly Mick's drinking was excessive even by local standards.

The level of violence also began to increase. In our second house, we had a landline, and whenever Mick became violent Mum would try and call the police. On a few occasions while assaulting her he would rip the phone line from the wall so that she could not make any calls. On these occasions she would yell for me to run to a phone box to call the police. Most of the time the police would take so long to arrive that by the time they did, the fight had ended and the folks had kissed and made up!

Resentment for Mick had been building within me for years. The violence in the home was becoming too much for me. I began to take note of things that could be used as weapons in various parts of the house. Since violence could break out in any one of the rooms, I wanted to be prepared for the time that I was going to either fight back to defend myself or intervene to help Mum. There was already a baseball bat in the hall cupboard (which was kept there for security purposes), the kitchen drawer had a hammer and I kept an empty glass bottle in my room upstairs.

The night finally came. I'd just gone to bed, and as I lay there I heard the all too familiar sound coming from downstairs. Voices were raised, and the sound of Mick kicking off made its way upstairs. I'd had enough. I jumped out of bed, threw on my clothes, grabbed the bottle and headed to the top of the stairs. As I made my way to the top of the stairs, Mick's son, who had been staying with us, called out from his room. He'd seen me with the bottle and had worked out what was about to happen. On hearing his son's voice, Mick made his way upstairs to find out what was happening.

I'd stepped back into my room and placed the bottle back on the chest of drawers. Mick burst into the room and challenged me about the bottle. 'What do you think you're doing?' he asked, pushing me back towards the window. The adrenaline rushed through my body; I launched towards him with a flurry of left and right hooks. He was a big guy, and he tried to hold on to me and attempted to bite my hand as I held him in a headlock while punching him repeatedly with my other fist. The rest of my family must have thought I was being killed, because my younger sister, who was about eleven at the time, came running into the room and started laying into him with the baseball bat.

SHORT-TERM PEACE

This incident served as a catalyst to Mick and Mum splitting up for a period of time. It was the first time that this had happened. And for a season there was a degree of peace in the home. It was short lived, as Mick and Mum soon got back together, and before long he was up to his antics again.

One night he came storming into my room with a broken whisky glass as I was lying in bed. He'd obviously been mulling over the fight that had taken place a few months before. He began to threaten me, but I pushed him aside and he was so drunk that he just fell over and began to cry. All of a sudden the oppressor did not seem so intimidating. This time it was my turn to leave. I threw my work gear into a bag and made my way to a friend's house. It was about eleven thirty in the evening.

ROLLER COASTER

Life was soon to become a roller coaster of events. The following years were a combination of highs and lows and twists and turns. I went from one job to another, one relationship to another and lived from one friend's house to another's. Nothing was stable in those days; everything was transient. During the drinking sessions my moods and behaviour would be unpredictable. What would start out as a promising night full of partying and fun would often end in anti-social behaviour.

At times my dysfunctional living was too much for my Mum to tolerate. During these occasions I would be told to leave the house. As a result, I ended up renting flats in the west end of Paisley. Having my own place at sixteen and seventeen proved to be too much freedom. One of the flats I rented was in a tenement building. There were four floors and three flats on each floor. The constant parties, loud music and frequent disturbances were too much for the other tenants. They eventually signed a petition to have me evicted.

FAMILY RECONNECTIONS

Prior to leaving Barrhead, I was introduced to a friend of a friend. We got chatting and after a short while realised that we might be related in some way. My mate's friend was from a scheme in Paisley. My dad was from Paisley, and most of his family still lived there. It turned out that this guy's Mum was my dad's cousin. In effect we were second cousins.

When I eventually moved to Paisley, I reconnected with him and as a result was introduced to various cousins, aunts and uncles who hadn't seen me since I was born. There was an immediate connection and sense of belonging, and the family resemblance was uncanny, plus their lives were as chaotic and dysfunctional as my life was!

Actually, it was worse. A number of my cousins were heavily involved in the drug scene. One of them was a leader of the local Young Team in that area. My experience in this scheme was completely different to my experience in Barrhead. In Barrhead I had no connections and no protection; here, there was an immediate sense of belonging and protection. I didn't have to do anything; I immediately belonged. No one from the Young Team gave me any hassle because of my connections.

What I was observing in my family were the effects of at least three generations of addiction and poverty. My dad's parents were alcoholics, my dad and his siblings also became heavy drinkers and their children (my cousins) became not just drinkers but heavily involved in drugs and crime.

NO GLORY IN GANG LAND

While I was living in Paisley, news came to me that one of my cousins had been attacked and almost killed. He'd run out the house to help his brother who was in trouble with some guys from another part of the scheme. As he ran round the corner, a car raced towards him and ran him over, then reversed over him and then drove over him a third time. The car stopped and one of the passengers jumped out and struck him with a baseball bat. The guy jumped back in the car, and they sped off and left him to die.

When the news came to me, I was at my uncle's house. We didn't know if he was going to survive; all we knew was that he was on a life-support machine. A number of us went up to visit him shortly after the incident. He was still on the life-support machine, and he was heavily drugged up. He took my hand and in a faint voice thanked me for coming to see him and asked me to get the guys who did this to him.

My cousin, amazingly, against all odds, pulled through, although it took him a long time to recover from his injuries. While he was in recovery, he stayed away from alcohol; he had been warned by the doctors that drink and drugs could seriously put his life at risk. He kept free for a few months, but as his strength slowly recovered, he returned to the drink. He would come to the pub and sip Cokes while the rest of us were knocking back pints. Sitting by when everyone was having fun proved to be too much for him. I remember the night he ordered his first beer since the attack. Sadness settled over me at the time; he was lucky to be alive and he'd been given a second chance, but the old life was pulling him back in. He was found dead several years later; he died of a drug overdose.

BACK TO BARRHEAD

After a season in Paisley I returned to Barrhead and moved back into my Mum's house. She and Mick had broken up, and she was seeing someone else. Things had settled out in the home. Her new boyfriend, Terry, was a good guy. He liked a good drink but never had the same issues with violence. Terry was well connected; he was from a large family in one of the neighbouring towns.

Upon returning to Barrhead, things were different. I no longer walked about with the same sense of fear that I had in my younger days. I re-connected with an old schoolmate who was now living in a flat near my Mum's.

In the years that I'd been undergoing my changes, Steve had been going through his. He had grown up with really strict, adoptive parents. He was smart, had an outgoing personality and in many ways had everything going for him. Steve had ended up frustrated with the strict boundaries and flew the nest. His adoptive parents were devastated, but Steve was on his own journey of self-destruction.

He was staying in a flat with a few other guys, and narcotics were always on the go. Here Steve could stay out as late as he wanted, get up when he wanted and do what he wanted. Upon my return to Barrhead, I regularly spent time with Steve and his mates.

DOWNWARD SPIRAL

By the time I was eighteen, my life had spiralled completely out of control. While many of my peers were celebrating their eighteenth birthdays by an initiation to a pub or a club, I was immersed in a drink culture that went beyond party time. While many other eighteen-year-olds were leaving school and heading to university, I had fully qualified in the school of dysfunction and chaos. Many school associates would go out for a social drink; in the scheme there was no such thing as a social drink. You drank to get wrecked. Many young people, when they turn eighteen, are entering the world stage with hope and prospects. As an eighteen-year-old I was at the end of myself and felt there was no hope. There was no purpose, only desperation and dependency. When many young people turn eighteen, they leave home and go out and explore the world. At eighteen it seemed like I'd been to hell and back.

4

Losing My Religion

FOR many people in the schemes, being a Catholic simply means you are *not* a Protestant, you *do* support Celtic Football Club and you *do not* like the Queen. On the other side, if you happen to be born a 'Proddy', you know that you are *not* a Catholic, you *do* support Rangers Football Club, and for some mystical reason which forever remains unknown to you, you *do not* like the Pope. Walk through any scheme in the central belt and you are likely to see graffiti scrawled on walls, bus shelters and lamp posts with various slogans demonstrating these various expressions of cultural Protestantism and Catholicism.

Growing up in the central belt has a tremendous impact on a person's point of view. Religion is a strong influence; it is embedded deep within the culture, but more often than not, it is meaningless. Religion is passed down from generation to generation; it marks which tribe you belong to, influences which football team you support and usually determines which school you will attend. In many families it even determines who you will marry. Catholics marrying Protestants and vice versa, in some circles, is an unforgivable sin.

Most people grow up with these sectarian influences, accept them, promote them and do not even think about them. Very often they know nothing about the history, the politics or the beliefs of Catholicism or Protestantism, but they inherit the cultural bias and hostility.

EARLY DAYS

I grew up in a Roman Catholic family. My Mum's father in particular was deeply religious. His faith went beyond the sectarianism that I have just described. I remember hearing how, on one occasion, he walked out of a Celtic and Rangers match never to return because he witnessed a Celtic fan throw a glass bottle at a Rangers fan. He was a man of principles, and he was a praying man. He also liked a few beers and a gamble at the bookies. In many ways he was an average west of Scotland bloke with a genuine faith in God.

As a child I spent quite a bit of time at my grandparents' house. I would spend the summers out in the garden playing with toy garden tools in my own little plot of garden behind the shed. I would regularly attend chapel with my Gran and Papa (as we called them). Gran and Papa would not only take me to church, but they also encouraged me to pray. Whenever I was staying at their home, in the evening when it was time for bed, we would go up the stairs together and my Papa would get on his knees and pray. Having shown me what to do, I was then invited to join him, and together we would pray to God for his blessing on our family. This became the regular practice as each night before bed we would kneel down and pray.

Growing up in a Catholic family, you saw religion as something that was just there. You were always surrounded by gentle visual reminders. My grandparents' home had crucifixes on the wall, a painting of Lourdes, and statues of Jesus, Mary and Joseph. As you came in the front door, there was a small blessing fount which held holy water, and you did not have to look far for rosary beads.

CATHOLIC SCHOOL

School was the same. From day one in primary school we were taught the sign of the cross. We would pray before and after school dinner. We were also taught to pray the Lord's Prayer and the Hail Mary. Chapel services were carried out in Catholic schools and regular sessions of the Rosary were the steady diet of religious life.

We were also encouraged to pray to various saints. I remember one occasion in primary school where the head teacher came into the class and told us all a personal story. She had been at the beach and had lost her engagement ring in the sand. She was deeply upset, and after frantically trying to find it, she gave up all hope of recovering her engagement ring from the vast and unyielding sandy beach. However, she happened to remember that Saint Anthony was 'The Restorer of Lost Things,' so she prayed to him and immediately found her engagement ring.

Catholic school was also marked by various initiations into the Catholic faith. In early primary school we were inducted into the 'sacrament of reconciliation' otherwise known as having our 'First Confession'. This is where we would learn the procedure of confessing our sins to a priest.

The second major milestone is the sacrament of Holy Communion; halfway through primary school we would prepare for our 'First Holy Communion'. The final process of initiation is 'Confirmation', where a young person 'confirms' his faith in Jesus and the teachings of the Catholic Church. The ceremonies are performed with seriousness and grandeur. However, in my own case, upon returning home after the ceremonies, it was back to business as usual.

In Johnstone, Saint David's Roman Catholic School was on one side of the street and Cochrane Castle, a Protestant (non-denominational) school was situated at the other side. These schools finished at different times in order to reduce the risk of fights. The Protestant school would be let out ten minutes later when most of the Catholics should have been on their road home. Very often, the word would spread like wildfire around the school 'we are fighting the Proddies after school'. During these occasions the lads from the Catholic school would head over to the other school and lie in wait for them.

PRACTICING CATHOLICS?

Catholics will often say that although they are Catholic, they are not 'practicing Catholics'. This is a way of saying that while they do not completely reject the Catholic faith, they are just not putting it into practice. Their belief does not define their lifestyle. It's another way of saying that they are living in a way that is inconsistent with the teaching of the Church. I think this is one of the reasons why many Catholics are riddled with guilt. They know what they should be doing, but they have no desire to do it.

In my younger days my Mum would take us to chapel, but as we got a bit older this practice was phased out. Eventually, she would send us to chapel on a Sunday morning on our own, but I think that was more about getting the weans out of the house so they could recover from the night before.

My sister and I would go to chapel together; we would also be given 'money for the plate'. At first we would go to chapel and put the money in the plate. Eventually, we stopped going to chapel and spent the money on sweets. We'd then play in the park for the remainder of the time. Shopping trolleys from the supermarket proved to be a great form of entertainment. We would take turns at pushing each other through the streets in the shopping trolley at great speed. Eventually, we would just roll the shopping trolley into the burn which ran through the park.

You could say that in our home, in comparison to my grandparents' home, we were not *practicing* Catholics. However, at weekends all the typical badges of central Scotland Catholicism could be found: the Old Firm game would be on the TV, and the stereo would be blaring a mixture of Celtic football club songs along with a good dose of Irish Rebel music.

BELIEF IN GOD

As a child and into my early teens I'd always believed in God. While my belief in God did not always have an outward religious and spiritual expression, it was there. I would often stay with my grandparents at the weekends. As I grew older, my Papa stopped accompanying me to the bedroom for prayer time. I was old enough to pray on my own. I did for a while, but then stopped. Whenever he came upstairs to say goodnight, he would always ask me, 'Have you said your prayers?' My response was always the same, 'yes.' Of course, this was usually a lie.

Prayer never died completely. I would often pray when I really wanted something or when I really needed to get out of trouble. The latter would happen more often. Often such prayers would be accompanied by promising God that if he would 'get me out of this one' then 'I would not do it again.' I would usually forget my side of the bargain.

GOD, WHY DON'T YOU ANSWER BACK?

The practice of getting on my knees before God probably ceased at the same time as my Papa stopped praying with me. With no one there to monitor the process, praying on my knees felt silly. I also stopped praying out loud. I never, however, stopped praying within. Most nights I would lie awake in bed pouring my thoughts Godward. As the family circumstances worsened, my thoughts became silent cries for help.

I remember being quite intrigued on one of these occasions. Why does God never speak? Why am I the one doing all the speaking? Surely if he exists, he must be able to speak. Why does God not answer? Does he exist? Praying seemed to be a one-sided conversation.

RELIGIOUS EDUCATION

Like the non-denominational schools, Catholic schools had Religious Education (RE) as part of the curriculum. The difference in the Catholic schools is that RE is not just about informing you about religion; it also seeks to instruct you in the ways of the Catholic Church.

RE in school was an opportunity to skive. It was a class in which we could take it easy and have a bit of a carry on (actually, not much has changed in RE classes over the years!). My time in RE was spent chatting with my mate, stabbing each other with pencils, and trying to get the rest of the class to laugh.

I do remember at one point in RE being captivated by a particular question. It was not anything that the teacher was teaching that sparked the question. I think the question arose simply from the fact we were in RE and RE was all about God. The question that gripped me was this: 'If everything comes from somewhere, and God created everything, then who created God?'

I began to discuss this with the other pupils sitting next to me; they did not know the answer, so I decided to ask the teacher. The question met with her immediate dismissal. I would not be so easily put off, so I persisted with my line of reasoning. Clearly, discussion was not such an important part of RE classes in those days as I was quickly told to go and stand outside the classroom! Later on in life, I would discover that my question was not such a silly question after all. It is actually one of the crucial questions of philosophy.

I remember some local priests taking a school assembly. I don't think anything would have prepared the several hundred pupils for what was about to take place. The priests were there to plug the priesthood! We sat for an hour listening to their account regarding life in the priesthood. They sold it from every angle, from the nobility of the calling, the challenges of the calling to the perks of the calling. No matter how hard they plugged it, I'm sure every adolescent boy in that assembly was thinking the same thing: 'What, no sex, *ever*?'

One of the pressures of school life is the question of what we want to do with the rest of our life. It is no small question. Many choices have to be made towards this end, such as the subjects you choose, and the university course that you want to study. I had no idea what I wanted to do with my life. I enjoyed English and entertained the notion of becoming an English teacher, but I was too disengaged with the system to turn this from fanciful wish into reality.

One night as I lay in bed, I was turning over in my mind the question of what I should be doing with my life. To my horror, the visit from the priests came back to my mind. I remember trembling at the thought that perhaps I was supposed to become a priest. I quickly banished the thought to the outer regions of my consciousness. Becoming a priest was the last thing I wanted to do with my life.

While I was not a particularly religious young person, the fact that my life had this strange combination of social chaos and religious influence would often cause me to wonder what life was all about.

On one of these occasions I remember staring out my bedroom window. I was thinking about how hopeless things seemed. The mob rule of the streets and the challenges of the home life were weighing heavily upon my mind. As I was dwelling on these things, I began to wonder what life would be like if Jesus had come to earth in *my* life time, to *my* scheme. As I looked out at the grassy area across from my home and pictured Jesus sitting there and teaching the people of our community, I arrived at the conclusion that if Jesus were to be here today everything would be alright.

THE GOD WE IGNORE

The type of religion that many families experience in the west of Scotland is more a case of ignoring God than it is faith in God. His existence is sort of assumed, perhaps taken for granted, but he is expected to remain on the outskirts of our lives only to be called upon (or cursed) in times of trouble.

Occasionally, 'God' is brought out of the cupboard for display on special occasions such as christenings, weddings and funerals, but he is quickly banished as soon as the after-ceremony celebrations begin (after all,

God would only spoil the party!). The 'God' of western Scotland may come to us in the name of Christianity, but he is a distant God, a God who is far away and who does not interfere with everyday life, and we like it that way.

DETERMINING THAT GOD DOES NOT EXIST
As a teenager, as my lifestyle became more careless, I began to question my earlier religious teaching. If God existed, why did he not prevent our home life from deteriorating into chaos? Why did he never answer any prayers? Why was there so much crime and violence in the area?

As I think back, there was another reason why I rejected belief in the existence of God (which I was not aware of at the time). My own lifestyle choice was so far removed from God's standards (or even mainstream society's standards), that it was convenient for me to believe that he did not exist. If God existed, then I would be accountable for my actions. If God did not exist, I could carry on freely without worrying about consequences.

DEPTHS OF DESPAIR
The high life eventually becomes the low life. As the old saying goes, 'What goes up must come down.' The higher you go, the lower you fall. My nights of bingeing would be followed by tremendous come downs. I had no idea the damage I was doing to my emotional, mental and physical health, but the signs were beginning to show. The very substances which provided me with confidence during the highs became my tormentors during the lows. My closest friends became my worst enemies.

My body began to experience side effects, and I began to have anxiety attacks. During these occasions I would be gripped by a deep sense of fear. More often than not, if I was not drinking, I would feel extremely anxious and the only thing that calmed me down was alcohol. At one point I had to drink at least four bottles of beer a night just to feel normal. These would not get me drunk; they would just let me feel calm and perhaps get some sleep.

One morning I awoke to a terrible come down, and images of the previous night's antics began to flash before my eyes. It had been another night of too much alcohol and fighting. I'd been drinking with one of the neighbours, but for one reason or another we'd ended up arguing. I remember being dragged out of the flat and locked outside the close, but I was raging because my carry out was inside the flat. I'd managed to grab a pool cue on the way out, so I just started caving the close window in with the heavy end of the cue. As I lay in bed recalling the event, I remember calling out, 'Oh God, please help me!' The silence was deafening. Immediately a thought filled my mind: 'God does not exist, remember?' That's right, I thought, I don't believe in God anymore.

5

Steps Determined by Destiny

~~~~~~~~~~~~~~~~

A sense of regret began to overshadow me. My life seemed to be an endless story of wasted opportunities. I was caught in a web; the more I struggled to break free, the more entangled I became. I'd tried to break my drinking habits several times, but each time ended in failure. Hope was evasive, and thoughts of suicide flashed through my mind. After a bout of drinking, when I eventually sobered up, I would be left in a state of anxiety and depression for days.

SEARCHING FOR HOPE

I'd moved back into my Mum's house, and one day, just after lunch time, whilst my Mum was at work and my brother and sister were at school, I'd reached a stage where I knew I needed help. I realised I was not going to be able to sort things out on my own. I felt a strange desire to read a Bible. I had a vague recollection that we had a 'Holy Book', which resembled what may have been a Bible, *somewhere* in the house. Being Catholic, we had all sorts of religious paraphernalia in the house, but rather than being highly visible and on display as they were at my grandparents' house, they were stashed away in a cupboard or drawer.

I went over to the storage unit at the back of the living room. I opened the cupboard and raked through countless useless items in search of a Bible. The cupboard was full of dead batteries, old keys and adapters for things that no longer worked. I knew that this was where the religious stuff was also kept.

A DIVINE COINCIDENCE?

As I raked through the cupboard, I found holy water, confirmation candles, crucifixes and a prayer book, but no Bible. What I had thought was a Bible was simply a book on Catholic liturgy, and most of it was completely unintelligible to me. I gave up my search and resigned myself to the fact that there was no Bible in the house.

A short while later my sister came home from school. She would have been in first or second year at the time. Upon coming through the front door, the first words that came out of her mouth were, 'The Gideons were at school today, and they gave me this Bible.' A strange feeling came over me; it was like fear mingled with intrigue.

I tried to play it cool. I wanted the Bible, but I did not want it known that I had any interest in it. I made some sarcastic comments about 'Bible bashers' and in a dismissive tone of voice asked her to 'show me the book anyway'. 'What's all this about?' I sneered, flicking through the pages.

As I opened the first few pages, I glanced at the words on the page and found myself trembling with fear. The words on the page grabbed my attention in a vice-like grip: 'Where to find help when in time of need ... Desperate (at your wits' end) ... Distressed or troubled ... Tempted to commit suicide ... Drink abuse ... Drugs abuse.'

What on earth is going on? I thought to myself. These are the very issues that I am facing. How can this book, which is thousands of years old, speak to these modern problems? What does the Bible have to say about these issues? This is supposed to be a religious book.

Up until now, I'd considered religion to be something that was completely irrelevant to everyday life. I had no idea that the Bible spoke right into the very questions and struggles of human existence. The Bible lacks the polished nature of a human religious ceremony. It is gritty because life is gritty.

I'm not sure that my sister ever did get her Gideon Bible back. As I reflect on this situation, although I did not fully understand it at the time, I now understand that Heaven's hand was upon my life. God's hand had always been upon my life, but now eternity was beginning to break into the natural realm. The incident with the Bible did not cause me to drop to my knees and turn to God, but it did create within me a sense of awe and fear. Later on, when I did turn to Christ, I would remember this incident and it would reinforce the fact that God was ordering my steps.

At times when I would feel really low, I would turn to the little red Gideon New Testament and Psalms. To be honest, most of the time I had no idea what it was talking about. One day I turned to the Book of Revelation, and I stumbled on the part which speaks about the final judgement. I very quickly understood the heart of this passage. There was a day to come when God would judge the entire world. The book spoke of people in white robes. I figured that these were Christians. It spoke of the condemnation of the wicked. I immediately knew which category I fell into.

RETURNING TO PAISLEY

Although I was occasionally consulting the Bible, very little changed outwardly. I was still drinking excessive amounts of alcohol, getting into fights and occasionally having encounters with the police. I was working with my godfather again and eventually moved into one of his flats in Paisley.

As I was getting ready to move back to Paisley, a woman who lived in the flat next door asked me if I wanted a dining room table. As I went to collect it, there was a stranger standing at her door. My neighbour wasn't in, but this woman was religious and was handing out leaflets about her religion.

She began to speak to me about 'God's promise' and asked me if I was interested in more information. I felt quite awkward talking to this religious woman in public, in a scheme that was not exactly known for religious sensitivity. I took a leaflet, shoved it in my pocket and headed back to my Mum's house.

THE LION AND THE LAMB

When I moved into my new flat, I came across the leaflet that I had been given. The message was based upon the following verse from the Bible:

> The wolf shall dwell with the lamb, and the leopard shall lie down with the young goat, and the calf and the lion and the fattened calf together; and a little child shall lead them.
>
> ISAIAH 11:6

This Bible verse really made an impact upon me. From what I could understand, it spoke of two things. It spoke of how things were *meant to be* and spoke of how things one day *would be*. It spoke of peace, but the world we experience is in conflict. In the world that I knew, families were in conflict, and communities were in conflict. The Bible verse spoke of a peace so great that even a lion and a lamb could dwell in harmony. The world I knew was a world of violence and danger. The world of this Bible verse was a world of peace and safety. I remembered that God had created the world like this in the beginning, and I became deeply aware of just how much people had wrecked God's world. I became aware of how I had wrecked God's world through my own selfishness.

The Bible verse also seemed to suggest that God would once again restore the world to the condition of perfection. My heart longed for this world, a world of peace and safety. A world untainted by evil and suffering. As I read the Bible verses over and over again and thought about the state of the world, I just knew that it wasn't supposed to be like this.

THE WEST END

My new flat was not much different from the old one. It instantly became a place for drinking sessions and revelry. I had started working at the roofing company again. Evenings would be spent drinking with the guys from work or my dad's side of the family or just simply drinking on my own.

I was living in the west end of Paisley, where many of my aunts and uncles were also living. The west end is on the outskirts of the town centre and leads into Ferguslie

Park ('Feegie'), where my dad's side of the family lived. It is a rough area, and in many ways it was like the scheme in Barrhead but with even less sense of community. The towering tenements gave it the 'lonely city' feel and the large numbers of criminals and drug addicts gave it a sinister atmosphere. All sorts went on in the west end of Paisley.

SEARCHING QUESTIONS
While my lifestyle remained the same, an inner spiritual quest had begun. Occasionally, while visiting charity shops, I would come across a book on Eastern mysticism or reincarnation. I began to consider the possibility of a non-Christian spiritual view of the universe.

Occasionally, I would spark up conversations about religion and philosophy with the folk I was drinking or working beside. Most people in the central belt tend not have these sorts of conversations. A piece of advice I was given when I went to the pub with the guys from work for the first time was, 'There are three things you never talk about in a pub: football, religion and politics.' These were personal matters which would likely lead to arguments and fights; it was best if a person's opinions on these issues were kept to himself.

One night while drinking with my uncle Rab, we sat listening to music and talking about everything and nothing. He was a Robbie Williams fan and had brought his latest CD with him. At this time in the late nineties, Robbie Williams was fighting his own battles with alcohol and drugs, and his songs reflected this. His songs also conveyed something of a deep spiritual search that was taking place within him at that time. His new album had several references to faith, Jesus and heaven.

This sparked a conversation about Christianity, and I was surprised at Rab's response. He told me that his sister, my aunt Mary, had become a Christian a number of years back. This surprised me; Aunt Mary was a party animal and, like the rest of us, was crazy with a drink in her. Mary was the last person I ever expected to go to church, never mind become a Christian. However, she and her partner had converted to Christianity and for a period of time stayed off the drink and away from all the madness that went with it. Rab began to tell me about the church. It was in the west end of Paisley, right next door to the pub where we all drank. The church was literally across the road from my flat. He confessed that he wouldn't mind going back to church, and before the night had ended, we agreed to go to the church together sometime. Rab and I never did make it to church together. We did make it to the pub next door though.

A LIGHT SHINING IN THE DARKNESS

The pub next to the church sold the cheapest pint in town. This was one of the reasons why it was filled with alcoholics looking for a cheap drink. All sorts of dodgy deals would happen in this place.

One dark winter's night, while drinking with a few of my uncles, we ran out of fags, and I agreed to nip over to my flat and get some tobacco. I was heading away from the pub when I noticed the little church building next door to the pub had its lights on. The gates were open, and it looked as if a service was on. Feeling quite confident since I had a bit of a drink in me, I ducked through the doors of the church.

I entered a foyer; the meeting seemed to have started. A door opened, and a burly guy with an Australian accent asked me what I wanted. I told him I was interested in finding out about the church. He handed me a Bible and a hymn book and directed me to a chair. What I observed was very different to the church I was used to. No altar, no crucifixes, no large crowds and no pomp and ceremony. Instead, there was a small group of people, no more than fifteen, sitting in a circle, and at various points someone would stand to pray what seemed like 'off the cuff' prayers. Having a wee drink in me and feeling quite jolly, I was tempted to stand up and give out a few thoughts of my own since that seemed to be the name of the game. I'm not sure which one it was, but common sense or divine intervention must have kicked in because I remained pinned to my chair!

After the meeting a few of the folks came and spoke to me; they all seemed very nice. There were even a couple of good-looking girls who were around my age. Within a matter of about twenty minutes I was engaged in conversation about Roman Catholicism, baptism and the Trinity. I'm sure they were not used to guys from the streets coming in and asking questions about their theology! I was warmly invited to attend the gospel meeting the following Sunday. After the meeting I headed back to the pub having collected the tobacco.

I awoke the next morning with a stinker of a hangover. My mind replayed the previous night's activities. No fights that I could remember; this brought a sense of relief. Then I remembered the visit to the church. Oh no, what an idiot, I thought to myself. What did you go and do that for? A sense of embarrassment came over me. As I lay there thinking about it, I remembered that although I was a little drunk when I went into the church, and although I was quite talkative, I hadn't actually made a drunken fool of myself. I remembered the invite to the gospel meeting; I decided it was safe to give it a shot.

CONFRONTED WITH THE GOSPEL

The following Sunday seemed to come round quite quickly. I remember sitting in my flat at 6:10 pm, psyching myself for the evening service that started at 6:30 pm. I was apprehensive, perhaps even fearful. I entertained the thought of not going at all. For some reason I decided to stick with it, and I made my way to the church hall.

As I made my way up the steps and through the door, a tall, skinny, silver-haired man greeted me at the door. I remembered him from my previous visit. I made my way into the main hall; as I walked towards a seat, one of the girls, who I recognised from my previous visit turned round and smiled. 'Nice,' I thought to myself. Others came in, and a few nodded and smiled as they took up seats beside me. These people seemed very warm.

The meeting kicked off with prayer and some hymns, and after about twenty minutes a very elderly man made his way to the front of the church. He was very soft spoken, even monotone, but two very clear things stood out from his message. They impacted me at the time, and I can remember them clearly. In his message he spoke about someone whose life had been gripped by alcohol and hectic living and how this person had found Christ. This story affected me on several levels: he had just described my life, he was talking about this in church (is church not where we do religion?) and he was implying that this Jesus could change lives.

He concluded his message with an appeal. He emphasised the need for everyone to 'receive Jesus Christ as their personal saviour' and urged anyone present who had not made Christ their saviour to do so as a matter of priority. This is a set up, I thought to myself. I looked around this hall of approximately twenty people; they all looked at home, as if they were a part of this thing. This guy must know that I am the only one in here who doesn't belong in this gig. This sales pitch is aimed at me! The old boy who was preaching made a beeline for me as I was leaving. After a few courtesies he handed me a leaflet which was entitled *Enter through the Safe Door*. I took the leaflet and headed home.

BACK TO DARKNESS

In the following few days I heard that there was some dodgy vodka getting sold quite cheaply in Ferguslie Park. The vodka was nicknamed 'a bottle of who are you looking at?' because after drinking enough of it that's what people began to shout at each other. This particular brand of cheap vodka was renowned for sending people off their heads and sparking all sorts of arguments and fights.

The following weekend we bought several bottles of this vodka. We kept it at our various homes and would head out to the pub only to return later to make a dent in the vodka. As we were in the pub, Jim, a young guy about my age, joined our company. He seemed alright, so after a few beers we invited him back to my flat.

The drinking carried on into the early hours of Saturday morning. We awoke on Saturday afternoon and began drinking straight away. The stereo had been playing constantly, and I had only a limited selection of tunes. Jim suggested that we head down to his sister Anita's house to get some more music. It sounded like a plan, and I headed down with him while the rest of the folks carried on with the drinking.

We went up a close just a few doors down and made our way up the stairs and into his sister's home. He introduced me to Anita and explained why we were there. Her own stereo was blasting out some music, and as she began to search for some tapes and albums, she turned the stereo down and apologised for the music as it was 'Christian music.' It turned out that Jim's sister was a believer in Christ.

The rest of this weekend turned into a non-stop session. I am not sure how many bottles of vodka were bought that weekend, but it was a crazy amount. A lot of the time was spent in Ferguslie Park, and by the time Sunday night came, I began to make my way home to the west end. However, rather than go straight home, I decided to pop in and see my new friend at his sister's flat.

Jim was not in, but his sister invited me in anyway. He'd gone to the police station because Anita's husband had been arrested by the police for outstanding warrants. As I sat on her couch, we began to speak about God and a strange thing happened. I began to feel the effects of alcohol wear off. I seemed to completely sober up. As Anita was talking about her faith, she said the following words: 'There comes a time when God gives you an opportunity to get things right with him. We should take that opportunity when it comes because we may never get another chance.' These words cut me like a knife.

I began to wonder if the various 'coincidences' I had been experiencing were actually God's way of seeking to get through to me. Before I left Anita's house, she gave me a Bible since I no longer had the little Gideon New Testament.

6

From Chaos to Christ

I awoke in a terrible state. I tried to sleep off the hangover, but no matter how hard I tried, I could not sleep. I had no money left, so heading out to the pub or buying a carry out was out of the question.

I was completely restless, and no matter what I tried to do, I couldn't escape this unsettled feeling. I tried watching TV, making a cup of tea, even occupying myself with household tasks, but the sense of unrest only increased. I felt like going out of the house, but there was nowhere to go.

BROUGHT TO REPENTANCE

I went to my bedroom and picked up the Bible that Anita had given me and the leaflet that the old preacher had given me. I flicked through the leaflet; it spoke about Jesus being the only 'safe door' and that in order to be saved we need to enter through this door. It was all a bit too metaphorical for me, but there was a prayer at the back of the leaflet. It was a prayer which invited the reader to trust in Jesus Christ as Saviour and Lord.

I knew what I had to do; I needed to ask Jesus into my life. I immediately fell on my knees and began to cry out to

God. I poured out my heart in a confession of sin, telling God how sorry I was for the mess I had made of my life. Instead of just asking him to help me and promising to try and do better, I prayed the prayer on the back of the leaflet. I did not know it at the time, but I was praying what is known as the 'sinner's prayer':

> Lord Almighty, have mercy on me, a sinner. I believe in you and that your word is true. I believe that Jesus Christ is the Son of the living God and that He died on the cross so that I may now have forgiveness for my sins and eternal life. I believe in my heart that you, Lord God, raised Him from the dead. Please, Jesus, forgive me for every sin I have ever committed or done in my heart; please, Lord Jesus, forgive me and come into my heart as my personal Lord and Saviour today. I give you my life and ask you to take full control from this moment on; I pray this in the name of Jesus Christ.

After some time praying, I arose from my knees feeling a little calmer. I decided to pack a bag and head to my Mum's in Barrhead. I threw some clothes in the bag, placed the Bible in the bag and headed out. I had no idea how much my life was about to change. Although there was no obvious or immediate change (I did not expect there to be any), I really did not realise what I had just done. I had called upon the name of Jesus in repentance and faith and asked him to come into my life. The direction of my life was about to be set on a radically new course.

As I began to walk through the town, I gave no more thought to the prayer I had made earlier in the morning. I headed towards my godfather's house to borrow some money for a bus from Paisley to Barrhead. As I neared my godfather's estate, a strange thing happened. I looked past the concrete paving and man-made houses and caught a glimpse of the natural world, which, to be fair, there was not much of. The natural shrubbery and grass caught my attention. There was nothing outstandingly beautiful about it, but all of a sudden I seemed to become aware of God's existence. In my heart I said 'God, I *know* you are there.'

THE GLORY OF THE LORD

I arrived at my godfather's house, and I was given some lunch along with the money I needed to get the bus home. After lunch, I made my way to the bus stop at the end of the estate. The bus arrived; I stepped onto the bus, took a seat and spent the journey looking out the window. It was January, the skies were bright blue, the sun was dazzling. All of a sudden I began to feel something. While I struggled to describe it at the time, a feeling of love, joy and peace began to wash over my entire being. Fear, guilt and shame evaporated and love filled its place. It was so strong, I had to resist the urge to jump up and hug all of the people on the bus! I looked out the window again, and the whole world seemed to have been transformed. Every part of creation seemed to radiate with life and light. I became deeply aware of Jesus. I could not see him, but I knew it was him; I needed no introduction.

I didn't really understand what was happening; I had never heard of such experiences or that they were even possible. Having lived for years in a place of fear and shame, this was like leaving hell and entering heaven. Unable to explain what was taking place at the time, I now realise that my eyes were being opened to the glory of God.

> 'Holy, holy, holy is the LORD of hosts; the whole
> earth is full of his glory!'   ISAIAH 6:3

People often talk about conversion experiences, mockingly, as 'seeing the light'. However, there is a degree of truth in this. The Bible describes the unbeliever as a person who is blind. This does not means that person cannot physically see, it means they cannot see spiritually:

> The god of this world has blinded the minds
> of the unbelievers, to keep them from seeing
> the light of the gospel of the glory of Christ,
> who is the image of God.   2 CORINTHIANS 4:4

The Bible does not only teach us about God, it also teaches us about the devil (the 'god' of this age). The devil is not God's equal. He is a created being, a former angel, created by God, who rebelled against God and lost his place in heaven. The devil is a spiritual being who hates God and who desires to destroy humanity. It was the devil who tempted Adam and Eve to sin against God in the garden of Eden (Genesis 3), and it is the devil who leads people astray today (Revelation 12:9). It is the devil who blinds people and prevents them from seeing the beauty of Jesus. It is only God who can remove this blindness and He does this through the gospel.

Although I did not understand it at the time, I now know that God was opening my eyes to see the beauty of

Jesus and one of the first ways I began to see his glory was in the creation. The whole world seemed like a massive signpost pointing to a creator God.

HEAVEN ON EARTH?

I struggled to make sense of my new experience but I had no words to express it. All I knew was that I needed to get back to the church on King Street as soon as possible. If anyone knew what was going on, surely they would.

After a few days in Barrhead, I returned to Paisley. At times the sensation I experienced on the bus would return. It could happen while in a room with several people, or it would happen when I was on my own. Suddenly and without warning, my heart would begin to burn with a sense of warmth and love. Very often it would happen when my thoughts turned towards God.

I began to attend the west end church at King Street on a regular basis; I'd be at the Sunday morning and evening meetings and the midweek Bible studies. Very often in these meetings I would experience an overwhelming sense of God's presence. At times I had to hold back from shouting out God's praises, so great was the joy in my heart.

I still hadn't spoken to anyone about my experience. I was still unsure of what was happening to me; at points I wondered if I was going mad. In the church meetings there was no outward evidence that anyone else was experiencing the same thing that I was, so I kept it to myself. Looking back the only words I can think of to describe my experience is that it felt like heaven drawing near. I remember attending church one night and singing the following stanza from a hymn. The words seemed to encapsulate my experience:

> *Heaven above is softer blue,*
> *Earth around is sweeter green;*
> *Something lives in every hue*
> *Christless eyes have never seen*

What is that brought about this new reality? The first few lines of the hymn explain it well:

> *Loved with everlasting love,*
> *Led by grace that love to know;*
> *Spirit, breathing from above,*
> *Thou hast taught me it is so.*

In other words it is the Holy Spirit of God who leads us to a saving faith in Christ.

SAVED?
Not long after I began to go to the church, an older woman approached me and handed me a leaflet and asked me if I had been saved? The leaflet was also entitled 'Are You Saved?' I had no idea what it meant to be 'saved', but she obviously had her doubts regarding my profession of faith. All I knew was that God had become very real.

Although I didn't understand the question the woman was asking me, I now appreciate that she was in fact asking me a very important question. One of the main differences between the evangelical church and the Roman Catholic church is the teaching about salvation (salvation means to be saved from sin and God's eternal judgement.) In the Roman Catholic church, I was taught good people go to heaven and bad people go to hell.

The Bible, on the other hand emphasises that no one is good by nature, 'for all have sinned and fall short of the glory of God.' (Romans 3:23) Consequently, because we are sinners, we all must face death, 'For the wages of sin is death.' (Romans 6:23). If this wasn't serious enough, after death we face judgement, 'it is appointed for man to die once, and after that comes judgment.' (Hebrews 9:27). Because we are sinners, the judgement is bad news. No one will be considered righteous on their own merit. This is why the woman was asking if I had been saved. True Christianity is not just about trying to be a better person, true Christianity is about being saved from our sin and the wrath of God.

Roman Catholics are also taught that a person can never really know if they are saved. The Bible on the other hand teaches that a person can know here and now whether or not they are saved. We can know here and now whether or not we are going to heaven. The Apostle John wrote, ' I write these things to you who believe in the name of the Son of God that you may know that you have eternal life' (1 John 5:13).

In other words, the Christian faith is not about trying to be a good person in the hope that God may let us in to heaven. The Christian faith offers us assurance, the deep confidence that we will not be condemned by God on the Day of Judgement. How is this possible? It is only possible because salvation is not a wage for good works, it is a gift for the undeserving. Jesus has paid the price for our sins and it is only by trusting him that we can be saved: 'For by grace you have been saved through faith. And this is not your own doing; it is the gift of God' (Ephesians 2:8)

So when the older woman was asking me, 'Are you saved?', she was asking me if I was assured of my salvation. Many evangelical churches no longer do this. They no longer expect new believers to find assurance for themselves. Very often people who are interested in becoming a Christian are simply told to pray the sinner's prayer, and the minister declares them to be saved. This is counter-productive, it is much better for a person to be assured of their faith by the Holy Spirit and through genuine faith in the Word of God. Too many people who make a profession of faith have only the assurance of a preacher but lack the assurance of God's Spirit. The apostle Paul taught that assurance is brought about by the Holy Spirit: 'The Spirit himself bears witness with our spirit that we are children of God.' (Romans 8:16) Although I had responded to the gospel and seemed to be aware of God's presence, I did not have this assurance which the bible spoke about.

BAPTISM

The church I had stumbled upon is what is known as an evangelical Church. The church had a strong emphasis on teaching the Bible; it was non-charismatic (therefore naturally cautious of religious experiences), and it stressed the great importance of preaching the gospel. Visitors to the church would be left in no doubt regarding what the church believed. A clear message, warning of hell, proclaiming the crucified saviour and an exhortation to trust in Jesus and be baptised was at the heart of the church.

After His resurrection, and before He ascended to heaven, Jesus gave his disciples the following instructions:

> Go therefore and make disciples of all nations, baptizing them in the name of the Father and of the Son and of the Holy Spirit, teaching them to observe all that I have commanded you. And behold, I am with you always, to the end of the age.　　MATTHEW 28:19-20

Baptism is one of the issues that many churches are divided over. Churches do not agree on *who* should be baptised (some argue that only believers should be baptised whereas others will baptise the children of believers before they profess faith); *how* people should be baptised (Sprinkling, pouring or immersion) or *what* baptism accomplishes (is it only a symbol or does baptism impart grace?). Leaving aside the theological arguments for the various understandings of baptism; at a very basic level baptism speaks of the washing away of sin, new life in Christ and union with Christ.

The evangelical church held to believer's baptism, and only those who had been baptised by full immersion could become a member of the church.

As soon as I learned about baptism, I was eager to be baptised. I approached the elder of the church and told him that I would like to be baptised. He asked me why I wanted to be baptised. 'Well,' I said, 'you know that "saved" thing? Well, I think that has happened to me.'

'What makes you think that?'

At that time I was not very articulate, so I awkwardly told him that 'one day I was on a bus and felt blessed'. My confession of faith clearly lacked some essential theological elements! However, after a few weeks of baptismal classes, the church accepted my request for baptism and membership.

THE STRUGGLE FOR FREEDOM

I did not transition into the Christian life easily. I often hear about conversion stories where people are instantaneously delivered from all addiction and sin. This was not my experience. I struggled with what felt like a losing battle with my way of living for almost a year. At times I would feel that I was making progress, but no sooner would I take two steps forward than I would take ten steps backwards.

Rather than drinking every other night of the week, I would stay clear of it for weeks but then go on drinking bouts that could last for two or three weeks. My mate Steve had moved to Greenock, and whenever I was fed up, I would cash my giro, catch a train, and head to Greenock for some heavy drinking.

I'd blow my giro on drink, then he'd get his giro and we'd spend that on drink too. We would then head to the Social Security Office and give them a sob story in order to get a crisis loan. It was common practice in those days to apply for a loan, which was intended to help people in crisis. We would make up stories about losing money, family members dying, power cards running out (causing our freezer to defrost and all our food to go to waste). If the story was convincing enough, and if you hadn't applied for a loan for some time, they would grant your request and give you a giro, which you could cash in and buy drink or whatever else you needed it for.

Whenever I headed to Greenock, it was the same story: I'd meet Steve, we'd hook up with some girls and we'd spend days on end drinking heavily. At the end of the sessions the guilt I experienced was unbearable. I knew this behaviour was incompatible with new life in Jesus, but I didn't know how to break free.

On one occasion I had been in Greenock for about three weeks when I decided to phone the elder of the church to let him know where I was and that I'd be home in a few days once I'd cashed my next giro. To my surprise, he offered to come and collect me in the next hour. I agreed to his suggestion. I felt awful and just wanted to get back home.

The elder appeared within the hour, dropped me off at my flat and handed me a bag of groceries he had purchased for me. I was touched by his kindness. He obviously knew I had been out on a 'bender' and had blown all my cash. There was no condemnation from him at all. He also took me back to his house, where his wife made lunch for us. As I sat in his living room while lunch was being prepared, he appeared with a Bible, handed it to me on his way through to the kitchen and simply said, 'I assume you will need some spiritual food.'

The elder and his family, along with other members of the church, were a tremendous support to me in the early days of my conversion. Had it not been for his determination to persevere with me, I'm not sure I would have made it through this rocky period. As well as providing practical support, he would meet with me on a weekly basis to study the Bible in order to help me grow and develop my Christian walk.

A DESIRE TO SERVE GOD

The church was part of a wider network of Christian churches with branches all over the world. Consequently, we would have speakers from different fellowships (usually just the Scottish ones) come and speak at our church. One of these speakers was a guy from the Greenock branch. He had just returned from a mission trip in China. The Chinese mission trip involved smuggling Bibles into China, and he told several stories of missionaries being caught with Bibles and arrested. I was hooked. Getting jailed for Jesus sounded great!

I moved into a bed-sit in Paisley that was owned by a Christian. The house had six rooms which were mostly rented out by Christians. Moving here helped surround me with a Christian influence, and it also gave me exposure to Christians from different denominations as well as various Christian ministries.

A couple of the guys worked for an organisation called Teen Challenge. Teen Challenge is a Christian organisation that helps people struggling with addiction. The guys were based in a rehabilitation centre in Kilmacolm called the Haven. One of the guys asked me if I would be interested in becoming a volunteer with Teen Challenge. I wasn't working, so I agreed to visit their rehab centre and bus ministry. However, I was still struggling to overcome smoking and drinking myself; the reality is, I should have been in rehab as a client, not as a volunteer!

ATTEMPTS AT FREEDOM

The smoking was really getting to me; I tried desperately several times to break the habit. I was quite a heavy smoker, sometimes smoking twenty to thirty cigarettes a day. I was unemployed and could not afford the cost, so I often ended up smoking cheap tobacco instead.

One evening a visiting speaker came to the church and during the course of his message shared, in a powerful way, how he had given up smoking. One day he was sitting on a bench outside of a church and could hear hymns being sung. He felt convicted about his smoking. He got out his pack of cigarettes, took out a pen and paper and wrote the Bible verse, 'If anyone is in Christ, he is a new creation, old things have gone, and everything becomes new.' He stuffed the Bible verse into the cigarette packet and tossed it in a bin. He then walked away, never to smoke again. This inspired me. I'm not sure how many times I tried this, but each time within about half an hour I'd be out in the street trying to find my discarded packet of fags!

DEEPER DEALINGS

Becoming a Christian did not immediately set me on a path of peace and rest. If anything, it launched me into a war. There was a battle going on, and I felt my life being pulled in two opposite directions. On the one hand, there was the life I knew, a godless and self-indulgent, painful, yet comfortably familiar life of sin. On the other hand, there was the comforting hope of eternal life, but the pathway seemed to be overgrown with thorns. There was a call to righteousness, but the standard seemed beyond my grasp.

I confessed Jesus as Lord and Saviour, but I had no real abiding assurance of salvation. There was no victory over sin. My conscience was plagued by a sense of guilt and each time I turned from God to find refuge in the things of the world, the call of God would haunt me in the midnight hours.

One night I lay in bed reading the Bible; I was troubled by my lack of assurance of salvation. Was I truly saved from my sin and preserved for heaven? These thoughts turned over in my mind as I read through John's Gospel. As I stared at the text in front of me, one of the verses struck me like a jolt of electricity: 'Whoever believes has eternal life.' (John 6:47). The words seemed to come alive and imprinted themselves upon my mind.

I randomly turned the pages to another part of the Bible; I had no idea which part, but the words continued to grab my attention. My eyes fell upon a piece of scripture, and to my horror, it was like looking into a mirror and seeing a marred reflection looking back at me.

> The dogs have a mighty appetite;
> they never have enough.

> But they are shepherds who have no
>   understanding;
> they have all turned to their own way,
> each to his own gain, one and all.
> 'Come,' they say, 'let me get wine;
> let us fill ourselves with strong drink;
> and tomorrow will be like this day,
> great beyond measure.'
>
> (ISAIAH 56:11–12)

These words cut to the very centre of my being. I saw my sin for what it was: rebellion against God. I saw myself for what I was: selfish, hedonistic and rebellious. The fear of God gripped my entire body. I fell trembling to the floor and cried out in repentance, pleading for God to have mercy. The sense of eternal judgement was very real, and I expected to be immediately and forever consumed in hell's flames.

As I cried out to God in deep anguish and fear, an overwhelming sensation flowed through my entire being. I was physically trembling, and my mind and heart were caught up in the deepest and highest ecstasy I'd ever known. Words fail to fully describe the sense of joy and freedom that filled my entire being that evening. No wonder the apostle Peter spoke about it as 'joy that is inexpressible and filled with glory' (1 Peter 1:8).

I opened the Bible at another page; the text, again, coincided with what I was experiencing. As I read the following passage, it seemed as if I was being caught up in the very reality that the scripture was intending to convey.

> For you have not come to what may be touched,
> a blazing fire and darkness and gloom and

a tempest and the sound of a trumpet and a voice whose words made the hearers beg that no further messages be spoken to them. For they could not endure the order that was given, 'If even a beast touches the mountain, it shall be stoned.' Indeed, so terrifying was the sight that Moses said, 'I tremble with fear.' But you have come to Mount Zion and to the city of the living God, the heavenly Jerusalem, and to innumerable angels in festal gathering, and to the assembly of the firstborn who are enrolled in heaven, and to God, the judge of all, and to the spirits of the righteous made perfect, and to Jesus, the mediator of a new covenant, and to the sprinkled blood that speaks a better word than the blood of Abel.

See that you do not refuse him who is speaking. For if they did not escape when they refused him who warned them on earth, much less will we escape if we reject him who warns from heaven. At that time his voice shook the earth, but now he has promised, 'Yet once more I will shake not only the earth but also the heavens.' This phrase, 'Yet once more,' indicates the removal of things that are shaken—that is, things that have been made—in order that the things that cannot be shaken may remain. Therefore let us be grateful for receiving a kingdom that cannot be shaken, and thus let us offer to God acceptable worship, with reverence and awe, for our God is a consuming fire.

HEBREWS 12:18–29

This experience impacted me in several ways. I received a new awareness of God's presence, and I now seemed to have a new sensitivity towards how detestable sin is in God's eyes. It seemed as if I had been branded by the burning presence of God. The fear of God was birthed deeply within me, and the desire for his presence would lift me to new heights during prayer and worship. Nothing on earth could now compare with the reality of knowing God.

7

God's Plan and Purpose

THE new encounter with God left a deep impression upon me, but I still wasn't free. I had a greater desire to know God, live in holiness and serve Him, but I didn't seem to have the power. I needed help to know how to live the Christian life. I'd always been a reader, although, during my wilderness years I barely looked at a book. However, as soon as I became a Christian, people would give me books all the time. There was a local Christian bookshop and cafe in Paisley which was run by a local church. I'd often go there to pick up books and make connections with other Christians. During this period in my Christian life, I ended up with two books which made a deep impact upon me. One book dealt with the problem of the futility of *trying* to live *for* Christ instead of allowing Christ to live through us. The other book was similar; the emphasis was on the Holy Spirit filling us and transforming our hearts, souls, minds and desires. Both books were used by God to lead me to a fresh place of surrender. I gave up trying to be a Christian and asked Jesus Christ, by the power of His Spirit, to live through me.

The fresh surrender and trust in Christ led to a new season in my walk with God. There was no major spiritual experience, but there was closeness to God, a deep peace and a power to overcome desires which were contrary to God's will. The vice-like grip which smoking and drinking held upon me seemed to slowly evaporate.

In order to avoid temptation, I tried to get to as many Christian meetings as I could. If another church had a meeting on at a time when my own church didn't, I would go there. I discovered an outreach cafe in Paisley Town Centre which was called the Marah Drop-In. It was a ministry led by Stauros which was especially geared towards reaching out to people in addiction. Upon visiting the drop-in and speaking to the guy who ran it, John Kennedy, I quickly became involved in the work as a volunteer. The drop-in was open three days a week, but they also held a Stauros meeting every Thursday night. Stauros meetings are addiction support meetings which provide an opportunity for the guys to support each other, share their struggles, pray and be built up in the word of God.

During this period, God began to challenge me about putting things right in my life. It is one thing to believe that you have been redeemed and to repent of (stop and turn away from) certain sins; it is another thing to make retribution (to make amends for sins). There is no hard and fast rule about this, and we do not make amends to try and earn God's forgiveness. For some people, it would be impossible to make amends for every sin! I think the principle is that we should put things right whenever we can. If there are dangerous people that we have crossed, it may not be wise to intentionally seek them out, especially if they are involved in criminal activity; however, if God brings them across our path, we should make attempts to put things right.

One of the first examples of the Lord challenging me to put things right happened very early on in my walk with God. I'd dropped by the Christian bookshop to buy a CD. I was at the back of the shop looking through the CDs when a customer entered the shop and asked the assistant if the shop stocked Christening cards. I recognised the voice immediately; it was a woman's voice, and although I had not heard it for some time, it was a voice I had heard often. I was sure it was the 'provy woman' (a woman from the area who worked for Provident Loans Company). She had been my Mum's provy woman for years, and we would usually see her once a week for payments. I also knew her daughter who was the same age as me, but we had gone to different schools. I thought to myself, what is she doing in an evangelical bookshop? To my knowledge, she wasn't a Christian. Her religious persuasion was the least of my worries though; she had not only been my Mum's 'provy woman', but she'd been mine.

At the age sixteen I lied about my age and applied for a couple of loans, but I'd also defaulted on the payments. Moving away from Paisley had allowed me to slip off the radar. As I stood there, hidden behind the CD stand, I was tempted to stay there in the hope that she would soon leave the shop without noticing me. However, I had a strong sense in my gut to go and speak to her. However, I reasoned with myself, *No way, man, I owe her money, I'm staying right here.* However, the conviction that I needed to go and speak to her would not leave; it only got stronger. Taking a deep breath and praying for wisdom, I made my way to the counter to strike up conversation.

'Sandra,' I said awkwardly.

'John!' she exclaimed in surprise, 'what are *you* doing in here?'

'I was going to ask you the same thing. I've become a Christian.' Sandra's face lit up, and in a matter of minutes she informed me that she, too, had come to Christ—although for her it was more a matter of returning to Christ. She also told me that her daughter, Louisa, had got involved in the heroin scene but after hitting rock bottom had come to Christ and was presently in one of Teen Challenge's rehab centres. We spent the next few minutes swapping stories, and I was totally blown away by the ways in which God seemed to be working.

As a result of meeting Sandra, I was able to reconnect with Louisa, and we exchanged stories. Louisa suggested that I visit her Mum's church, an independent Charismatic church in Beith. Sandra had got involved with church through her neighbour, who was a born-again Christian. Sandra really enjoyed it and had started travelling to the church regularly. God was really using Sandra at this point through her role as a 'provy woman', and because of her natural way with people. She was meeting with people who had real problems on a regular basis and had a prime opportunity to reach people. As she shared with her clients what the Lord was doing in her and Louisa's life, people started coming to church with her and getting saved. At this point, the church in Beith had a real buzz about it, and Sandra was a key reason for this; she was a natural evangelist.

By now, I'd visited the church in Beith a couple of times, but the Lord was convicting me about speaking to Sandra about the unpaid loans. Consequently, I called her and apologised about the fraud and defaulting on the loans—she was very gracious and was just glad that I was saved. I then made enquiries about the outstanding debt and was relieved to hear that it had been written off.

RUMBLINGS IN THE JUNGLE

At the time of my conversion, my Mum, along with my brother and sister, who were still at school, moved from Barrhead to Ferguslie Park. My Mum got a job in a pub in the town centre, where she met a guy from Somerset. A few months into the relationship an argument broke out between my Mum's partner and the next-door neighbour. However, it just so happened that the neighbour was related to half the scheme, and the following night, a large crowd gathered outside the house threatening to kill my Mum and my sister. My Mum phoned me looking for help. In the end it was decided that the best course of action was for my Mum and her partner to flee in the car to Somerset with as many possessions as they could fit into the car. My Mum, her partner, the dog and the video went to Somerset, and my brother and sister were dropped off in a taxi at my bedsit. It was then agreed that I would make arrangements with my godfather to go back to the house in broad daylight with the work's van to collect as many household items as I could.

Although the circumstances were disturbing, the sense of peace I experienced during this time was exceptional. The Lord was very close. Some people paint a picture which makes it seem like the Christian life is a constant mountaintop experience. It isn't, but there are seasons when the Lord draws very near; more often than not, this happens in the difficult times. Everything in our lives may be falling apart, but there is this deep sense that everything is okay, because the one who holds the world together is holding you together. The psalmist put it this way: 'God is our refuge and strength, a very present help in trouble. Therefore we will not fear though the earth gives way, though the mountains be moved into the heart of the sea, though its waters roar and foam, though the mountains tremble at its swelling.' (Psalm 46:1–3).

Plans were put in place for the children to stay with our gran while my Mum and her partner applied for housing in Somerset. As soon as things were in place, my brother relocated to Somerset, and my sister stayed with my gran until I could apply for a house. Initially, I intended to apply for a house in Paisley but decided it would be better to get away from some of the negativity associated with the town, so I applied for a house in Kilbarchan, a small semi-rural village on the outskirts of Johnstone.

During this time the Lord seemed to be working in my sister's life. She'd made friends with a girl in her class whose Mum went to the church which met in the same building as the church I was going to (Living Waters). My sister and her friend were in similar circumstances; they both had family members who had become Christians and who were encouraging them to place their trust in Jesus. My sister was also due to start work experience, and the only placement that was left was in a local Christian nursery. As a result of coming to church youth events, and conversations with me, and chats with each other, both girls made professions of faith, started to read their Bibles regularly and began attending church more frequently.

THE MISSION
While living in Kilbarchan, and caring for my sister full time, I became involved with a local outreach in Johnstone, The Good News Gospel Mission, commonly known as 'The Mission'. Missionary C. T. Studd said, 'Some yearn

to live within the sound of a church bell. I'd rather run a rescue mission within a yard of hell.' Studd's words sum up the work of The Mission perfectly. It was a community café which opened six days a week, fed the hungry, provided tea and coffee for the stranger and sought to help people socially, practically and spiritually. Most importantly it was proactive in sharing the gospel with all who came in contact with its work. While the mission was not exclusively set up to work with drug and alcohol abusers, they tended to be the primary clientele.

The Mission had been set up by a guy called Tommy Stewart, a former alcoholic who had been homeless on the streets of London but heard the gospel and was powerfully saved. Tommy was a wee guy with a huge heart. He was a powerful evangelist who had the ability to speak to people about Christ in the gentlest and most gracious tones whilst warning people of their need to be saved with the greatest urgency. He was fantastic with people on an individual basis, but equally an able gospel preacher and teacher of God's word.

The Mission hosted a gospel meeting every Friday night which was attended mostly by folks who were not Christians and who had a drug or alcohol problem, plus Christians from a variety of local churches who had a heart for local outreach. My first ever preaching engagement was at The Mission. I'd shared my testimony many times, and I'd ministered words of encouragement in various churches, but I'd never preached a full sermon. Excited, I accepted the preaching engagement and spent some time preparing a gospel message. As the date of the preaching engagement arrived, I was feeling stirred in my spirit. After a time of praise and worship, I got up and preached from the text: 'As it was in the Days of Noah, so it will be when the Son of man returns.' I passionately reminded the hearers that those outside of Christ are no different to the people in Noah's day who were living carelessly and rejecting God's salvation. I reminded them that unless we call people to follow Christ, the lost will perish on the Day of Judgement; therefore, our responsibility to reach people is very great. And with that said, I ran out of steam. My first sermon: fiery and urgent, all five minutes of it.

THE POWER OF GOD
While I was living in Kilbarchan and involved with The Mission, I was helping at the Welcome Bus in Paisley. The Welcome Bus was led by a missionary called Maurice Howson. Maurice had a real heart for people bound up in addiction, even though this was not the kind of background he himself came from. Maurice was one of the most encouraging Christians I had ever met; he always seemed to look for the best in people. The Welcome Bus received people from all sorts of backgrounds. One day, a young guy came on the bus—his name was Rab. As we got chatting, he told me that although he was living in Paisley, he was from Inverclyde, and that he was in a mess because of heroin. You could see it in his eyes— he was crying out for help. As I listened to him, I felt a prompting to contact the guys who run the Teen Challenge Outreach Ministry in Kilmacolm. Normally, there is a long waiting list, but on this occasion we were able to arrange an interview for Rab quite soon. The only condition was that he come to church weekly.

Rab was in a mess because he had a severe heroin addiction, but he wasn't on any medication. He was severely rattling. Rab was also a nice guy, which didn't help him when it came to feeding his addiction. As we walked through the Town Centre, he told me that other folk in his situation would think nothing of snatching a handbag from someone walking past, but he just couldn't bring himself to do that. Rab didn't just come to church weekly; he came to every meeting possible. He went to Stauros meetings, he came to The Mission in Johnstone—anything that was on, he'd be there.

When I took him to The Mission, I was really struck by the way that Tommy approached him. We sat at a table; Tommy brought over some coffee, sat with us and began to ask him what was wrong. Rab opened up to Tommy about his heroin addiction.

'What are you?' asked Tommy.

'A junkie,' mumbled Rab.

'No, you're not,' said Tommy gently, but firmly. I was expecting him to follow this up with a statement of Rab's value to God.

'You're not a junkie, you're a sinner,' continued Tommy. I couldn't believe it; if Tommy was trying to make Rab feel better, he didn't seem to be going the right way about it!

However, there was wisdom in Tommy's approach. Tommy recognised that Rab was convinced that his problem was his heroin addiction, and that his solution lay in getting free from the drug. Tommy was experienced enough to know that many folk in Rab's situation have not really come to understand their real problem, which is sin. And until they realise this, they will never be able to embrace the true solution, Jesus Christ. Tommy spent the next few moments explaining the gospel to Rab.

At some point Rab made a commitment to Christ, met with Roy Lees from Teen Challenge, was given an entry date in three weeks' time and was given a methadone script from the GP.

Rab was relieved to be given the script, but he felt that the dosage was too low. The GP had given him a daily allowance of only thirty-five milligrams. Even with the script, Rab was still a jittering wreck and complained that the dosage was not enough to hold him together.

There were a number of nights when Rab crashed on the couch in my flat in Kilbarchan. One evening I decided to have a Bible study with Rab and my sister. We were studying Romans 1, and there was praise and worship music playing softly in the background. Towards the end of the study, Rab exclaimed:

'I can feel this amazing peace. This is unbelievable—I feel so happy! I can't stop smiling.' I explained to him that what he was encountering was the peace of God. Rab said he had never felt like this in his life; he then boldly declared, 'If I feel like this tomorrow, I'm not even going to go and get my script.' Sure enough, the next day, the Lord's presence was still all over Rab, and he didn't go and get his script. In fact, he was methadone free for the rest of the week then he went into the Teen Challenge Programme.

At this stage in my Christian life, my whole world revolved around evangelism. Every day was spent witnessing to people who were bound in addiction. A lot of Christians who had been on the road for a long time seemed to be amazed at how easy I found it to engage people from the most broken circumstances in conversations about Christ. Many Christians were puzzled by the fact that the people I spoke to seemed to open up around me and receive many of the things I was sharing with them—even the challenging truths about the coming Day of Judgement and the need to repent and be saved.

Looking back at this period, I appreciate that there were a number of factors that made the evangelism so effective.

Although I had become a Christian, it was obvious that I hadn't been brought up in a sheltered, middle-class, Christian home. I looked and sounded like someone from the scheme; the only difference was, I was deeply into this person called Jesus. To folk from the scheme and to middle-class Christians, this made me something of an oddity. The very fact that I could relate to the people who were caught up in the craziness was one of the key reasons why their barriers would come down. They were speaking to someone who could empathise, to some extent, where they were at. I also had a real experience of the gospel. In other words, there was an authenticity in what they were hearing.

Another factor which enabled me to witness effectively to people was the deep compassion that God had put in my heart for folk who were in desperate circumstances. I felt their suffering. Members of the Salvation Army once complained to William Booth, the founder of the Salvation Army, that they had tried every possible method to reach a particular group of people, and every attempt had failed. Booth replied, 'Try tears.' In other words, our hearts must be gripped by empathy for those who are suffering. There were times, alone in my flat in Kilbarchan, when I would be led to pray for the people in the community. At times I would find myself weeping uncontrollably as I considered their lost condition.

When I first got involved with local mission among hurt and broken people in Paisley, one of the volunteers began to speak to me about 'a burden for the lost.' As he spoke about this burden for lost souls, I realised that this was the very thing that God had planted in my own heart. Empathy for people's social suffering is not enough—that will only lead us to social work. A burden for the lost will drive us to prayer and proclamation of the gospel. A burden for the lost will deepen our empathy because we will realise that drug addiction and poverty, as painful as they are, are nothing compared to the endless pain of an eternity without God. Helping people socially while ignoring their spiritual condition is not loving; it is actually the most loveless thing that a true Christian can do.

The further factor which made the evangelism so effective was the fact that I had absolutely nothing, from a natural perspective, to offer God. I was uneducated, unskilled, and lacking any real confidence in my own ability. I was shy by nature; when I first came into the church, I could barely hold a conversation with people. I was so aware of my own inadequacies that whenever I had to share a testimony publically, I was so terrified that the only thing I could do was completely rely on God. It is my observation that when God's leading, and the willingness of an individual to submit to the Lord's leading come together, the outcome is that the Lord will touch people through what is said. God can bring the people he is working on to our outreaches, but we need to be sensitive to His leading and pray for wisdom for the right words. As we speak to people prayerfully, the Lord will often take the words and touch folk's hearts. Sometimes we are unaware that this is happening, but at other times there is a very tangible sense that God is speaking.

This season of reaching out to people from the various schemes was a real high point in my Christian life. In my mind, this is what I wanted to do for the rest of my life. I wanted to serve God full time as an evangelist among people who were caught in addiction. However, God had other plans.

8

YMCA

IN 2001, my sister moved to Somerset in order to be closer to family. With no responsibility for being her full-time carer, I was now free to explore work opportunities. A pastor of a local church brought to my attention the fact that Paisley YMCA was recruiting a Christian trainee youth worker. Initially, I wasn't interested because it was only part-time; therefore, I assumed that the wage would not cover my rent and living costs. I also didn't really see myself as a youth worker. I had done some youth work: I'd been involved in helping at the church youth club which reached out to the Hunterhill Young Team. I decided to look at the job information. It turned out that although it was not full-time, it did have a decent pay; therefore, I'd be able to work the twenty hours and cover my living costs. With a number of people praying for me, I applied for the post and was notified within a short time that I was invited to an interview.

The day of the interview came. I was interviewed by Graham Curry, the youth development worker for Paisley YMCA and a female colleague of his from another project. I don't remember much about the interview, but I do remember one thing very clearly. There were two desks in the office, each with a computer. At one point Graham pointed towards one of the desks and said, 'And this will be your desk if you are the successful candidate.'

A desk! I thought to myself, what on earth do you do at a desk? I'd never worked at a desk in my life. And I hadn't used a computer since I'd left school, which at this point would be approaching five years.

The YMCA called me in for a second interview, and at the end of this Graham offered me the post. The job was varied; my job description was simply to meet young people's social, emotional, physical and spiritual needs. In practice this meant organising youth clubs, discos and holiday clubs. After a few months in the YMCA, I was more or less coordinating most of the clubs and activities for the older teenagers. While the YMCA worked with primary school children, my involvement was mostly with the older teens. The age range I worked with spanned from twelve to eighteen. Most of the young people were either from the town centre or the surrounding council schemes such as Dykebar, Hunterhill, and Ferguslie Park.

NEW MISSION FIELD

Part of my role was to develop creative ways to introduce the Christian faith into the youth activities at Paisley YMCA. I didn't launch into this straight away. I spent the first few months getting to know the young people. In reality, some of them were seventeen, and I was twenty-one, so I was really only a few years older than most of them. The experience I'd gained in working with people in drop-in centres proved to be helpful for youth work. It also helped that most of the young people were from the same area as me; consequently, there were not as many cultural barriers to overcome. In fact, some of the young people who came to the YMCA youth clubs were my younger cousins or nephews. That said, working with young people was new territory in many ways, and I had a lot to learn.

TEENAGE CHAOS

It was easy to assume that the world of these young people was a million miles away from the world of social dysfunction described in earlier chapters, but the reality is it wasn't. Many of the young people came from broken homes; others lived in run-down council schemes amidst the myriad of social problems already outlined in this book. It was the same world; the only difference was that these young people needed to be reached before their own lives slipped out of control whereas my previous work had been with people whose lives had already spiralled out of control. One is like rescuing people after they have slipped down the side of a cliff; the other is like trying to rescue them before they blindly make their way to the cliff's edge.

INTRODUCING THE GOSPEL

We started to introduce more structure into the youth clubs—the youth club was now a mixture of free time, where the young people could chat, play pool, order drinks and play on game consoles. As well as free time we introduced group games, challenges and quizzes. I also started to introduce short, sharp messages. Sometimes the message would be linked to a game we had just played; other times it would be a video clip or sometimes a Bible verse relevantly applied to their lives. In the early days, *Youthwork* magazine proved to be a lifesaver—it always included session plans and ideas for activities and games. In most cases I just took the idea and adapted it for my own situation. After one of these presentations, one of the young people stood up, cursed God, and stormed out of the café. This particular young person came from troubled circumstances. He had experienced the bereavement of a close family member; he had been permanently excluded from one school and transferred to another school because he had assaulted a teacher.

Many youth workers would come to the conclusion that any approaches to sharing the gospel which lead people to walk away from the activity in anger are a failure. They assume that effective methods are the methods which cause people to accept their message positively. However, the remarkable thing about this situation is that this particular young person was the first young person to make a profession of faith. Not only was he the first to commit his life to Christ, he became a catalyst which caused many other young people to seek Christ for themselves.

AN UNEXPECTED HARVEST

The work at the YMCA began to flourish, there was a good vibe among the staff and the young people were really connecting with the project. The youth office started to become an unofficial drop-in where young people would pop in at any time in the day just to say hello or to ask for some advice.

I received word that Teen Challenge USA was visiting a local church, and I thought that this would be a great event to take some of the young people to. I invited Michael, the young guy who had got upset at one of the first gospel presentations, and a couple of others. I told them that some guys from really tough backgrounds would be sharing their stories about how their lives had been changed. To my pleasant surprise, they all seemed up for it.

The meeting kicked off with some very exuberant praise and worship. I wondered how the young folk would feel about this—Gale and Jake seemed a bit embarrassed by the happy-clappy atmosphere, but Michael was in his element. He was clapping away like mad, singing the words and smiling at the others as if he'd been a Pentecostal his whole life!

The testimonies were excellent, and the gospel message was dynamic and engaging. They issued an altar call, and Michael grabbed a hold of Gale's hand—much to her embarrassment—and almost ran to the front of the church. Those who went forward were prayed for, and then guided to the back hall where they could be counselled, prayed for and led to Christ.

I spent a good part of the evening praying for Gale and Michael. I was praying that it was really the Lord who had laid a hold of them and that it wasn't just the hype and emotionalism of the meeting. I wondered how Michael would be the next day. He was supposed to be volunteering at our holiday club.

I expected Michael to either play down what had happened, or to be very quiet about the whole thing. I couldn't have been more wrong. That night, he'd gone home to his Gran's house and told her bluntly, 'I've become a Jesus person!' His Gran had faith in God, so she was very supportive of this decision. Michael came bursting into the YMCA on Monday and declared his new-found allegiance to Christ to everyone he met. People were stunned; Michael was the last person that anyone expected to become a Christian.

Michael's conversion had an immediate effect on the other young people. He was very open about his faith. He was a natural leader, only now, instead of leading people along destructive paths, he was leading people to Christ. One time he was walking through Ferguslie Park, and someone shouted down to him from the window of a third-floor flat, 'Hey, Michael, Jesus is up here!'

'Naw, He's no! He's in here,' he shouted, while pointing to his heart.

It wasn't just Michael's beliefs which changed; his attitude and behaviour changed too. He didn't become perfect overnight (who does?), but he turned away from a number of destructive tendencies. Even his placement supervisor at his Training for Work Project commented on the difference that she'd noticed in Michael's life.

GLIMPSES OF REVIVAL

Over the next few months, many of the young people started to express a personal interest in the Christian life. They started coming to various church events; they turned up at the youth office asking for Bibles or asking how to become a Christian. I had absolutely no idea what to do. In many ways the whole thing caught me by surprise. Although the staff prayer meetings focused on the salvation of young people, and although my own efforts to communicate the gospel were tireless, I never actually expected anyone (never mind a large number of young people) to make professions of faith.

While I had grown in my gifting as an evangelist, I was really inexperienced when it came to teaching and discipleship. One of the major problems we faced was the question of church. We were a para-church organisation, and not a very good one at that. Only a few of our volunteers were Christians, and the link between the YMCA and the local church had weakened a long time ago. The young people connected with the YMCA, but we were not a church, and some of the young people did not always feel comfortable in the churches they visited. But then, some of the churches we visited didn't feel all that comfortable with us either!

On one occasion, I took a number of young people and staff members to a Saturday night meeting held in a local evangelical church. The visiting speaker was led to abandon his prepared message (he literally threw his notes away) and instead preached a dynamic and Christ-centred gospel message. Consequently, one of our key leaders gave her life to Christ at the end of the meeting. However, on the way out the door, one of the young people swore, and a woman from the church got on his case straightaway. 'Hey, don't you use that language in here!' I could see he was feeling awkward (he actually hadn't meant any harm), and before I knew it I was jumping to his defence, saying, 'You need to chill out and just be grateful that this guy has even come to your church.' These kinds of scenarios were common. On another occasion, a pastor, who was ex-military, became completely exasperated by the behaviour of some young people I brought to his church. He found their body language, interaction with each other during the sermon, and their feet on the chairs a major distraction.

I had a problem. The young people needed to be discipled, and church is where this should happen, but not all of them were ready for church. God had it in hand, though, and brought along a new guy called David . David was from a run down housing scheme in Glasgow, had a criminal record that could sink a battleship but had been saved while travelling in Spain. David was not your typical youth worker, but he had a heart for folk from the schemes, and he could see that there was a work of God emerging. It was David who advised me that I needed to set up a Bible study to help the young people grow in their faith.

At this point, people began to come out of the woodwork. A guy from the States, who was over on mission with a local Bible Centre, came along and supported the work. He was great, a solid evangelical, with a wicked sense of humour and brilliant with young folk. David agreed to lead the Bible study, which was to be held on a weekly basis at the 'YM'. One key feature of our Bible study was the food that accompanied it. Every week would include a takeaway from the Chinese restaurant or buckets of chicken from KFC—generally speaking, there could be between twelve and twenty-five people on any given night. God provided the volunteers and the money. Funding the takeaway on a weekly basis was no small cost, yet every week money would come from various sources, usually from local Christians who had heard what was happening among the young people. The YMCA, and many voluntary projects, often struggle to recruit volunteers, yet at one point we had more volunteers and money at the weekly Bible study than any other activity which the YMCA was running. The reason for this was simple: Christian people sensed the Lord at work. They could see His hand on what was happening. When the Lord is moving, we don't need to rely on secular marketing techniques. He provides the people and the cash.

Michael continued to go to the local church where he had heard the gospel. This church was very active in outreach, so there was always something that we could take the young people to. During this time, Mary and Ian Esson, a Christian family from Paisley who were involved with the church, opened up their home on a regular basis for many of the young people from the YM. Mary would cook meals, and the young folk would be invited back for lunch. The hospitality of the Essons was an important factor in the life of these young people. There they were shown acceptance, grace and genuine Christian friendship.

CHURCH FOR THE UN-CHURCHED

In addition to the weekly Bible study, we held a weekly youth fellowship on a Thursday night which became known as The Flame. The Flame was more like a church service, only for young people. There was a time of praise and worship, a visiting speaker, and sometimes there would be a time of prayer. The talks at The Flame tended to be evangelistic or geared towards motivating the young people in their Christian life. Those who attended the meeting were a mixture of Christians and unbelievers, but they were all part of the same friendship group.

On one particular evening, Graham Curry was lined up to bring the message. Graham brought through a very strong message on the call of God, and God's purpose for his people. He spoke about a passage in Genesis in which the enemies of God's people were blocking their wells, and God's people had to dig new wells. Graham was passionately calling the people in the room to get to that place where God would pour out his blessing through them. He emphasised the fact that the devil blocks the well of blessing in our lives, but God desires to cleanse us and enable His Holy Spirit to flow through us.

As Graham invited the young people to respond to the message, a large number of young people walked to the front of the church to be prayed for. We had some visiting young people on this particular night, too. As Graham began to pray for folk, a number of young people began to tremble, shake and cry. One of the older teenagers, a guy who had a developing drinking problem, was completely overwhelmed as I stood praying for him. He was physically shaking from head to foot, and his face was lit up with joy. I asked him, 'What's happening to you?'

'God's coming into my life,' was all he could say.

The season of fruitfulness continued unhindered. Just when we thought that we had seen the last profession of faith, more young people would come along, and they too, would be drawn to seek Christ for themselves. Young people from the Paisley schemes were praying, witnessing to their friends, testifying to sensing the presence of God and experiencing answers to prayers.

TRAINING GROUND

I mentioned in a previous chapter that I hated school; consequently, I left school with very poor qualifications. Yet, as part of my job with the YM, I had to undertake some formal studies in youth work. I began a Youth Work and Theology degree around the same time that the young people were making professions of faith. Technically, I should not have been on the course, since I didn't have a credit-level Standard Grade or a Higher to my name. From a natural perspective, I was accepted on the course because it was vocational in nature, and I had demonstrated that I had some skills in youth work. I was returning as a mature student (equal opportunities and all that), and I'd convinced them I was at least able to string enough words together in a manner that resembled some form of prose. From a spiritual perspective, God opened the door.

My time on the youth work course was probably one of the greatest challenges I faced in my Christian walk. I was out of my depth socially, culturally and academically. Growing up in the scheme, I'd inherited an anti-intellectual and anti-middle-class bias—and theological college was full of intellectual, middle-class Christians! My anti-intellectualism had also been reinforced by the churches that I was associated with. The churches I belonged to placed a strong emphasis on the literal meaning of the scriptures, and the role of the Holy Spirit in helping us understand the text. Consequently, I was extremely impatient with the time spent engaging with this and that theory of scripture. By the end, we were given so many theories of scripture that no one could say with confidence what anything meant! To me, it seemed straightforward: God had sent his son to save us, and those of us who are saved are called to share this message with others.

My emphasis on salvation was connected to one of the other reasons I found theological college a nightmare: my real desire was to see people saved; consequently, sitting around all day discussing the significance of a comma in John's Gospel, from my point of view, was time that would be better spent being equipped for evangelism. The youth work studies were no better; it seemed that people would rather spend time discussing the sociological significance of youth subcultures instead of learning how to reach them with the gospel.

THE HARVEST FAILS

One of the challenges of being at college part-time was the fact that I was not able to invest as much time at the YMCA. Where once I was there almost seven days a week, my studies meant I was being pulled in two different directions. Not long after the course started, problems began to emerge in the work with the young people at the YM. The season of professions of faith, spiritual hunger and spiritual experiences was coming to an end. Overall,

I think it lasted for about six to twelve months. The work with the young people continued, but the emphasis on the things of God was never the same. Like a wave, it seemed to rise to a climax, only to come down with a crash.

At one point the whole youth group, along with one of the young people's family, turned up at church to witness him being baptised. This was the wave reaching its peak. I expected the whole youth group and the young person's family to get saved, but they didn't. Instead, there was a gradual season of decline. The most difficult part of observing the decline was the fact that many of the young people who made professions of faith soon turned away from God and ended up in disastrous circumstances. Some went to prison, others turned to alcohol and a few others got involved in the drug scene. Not everyone went to extremes; some just went and got on with life, but life without God.

Looking back, I can see there were a number of factors (and I don't think any one reason can be identified as being the key reason) why the blessing seemed to lift. For one thing, God is sovereign, and spiritual blessing is a sign of His grace. It is not a right and neither is it something that we should assume will be with us all the time. However, some of the factors that contributed to the disintegration of the work included weak connections between the para-church organisation and local churches, a major split within the local church that the young people were going to, and social pressures and bereavement experienced by the young people. For example, shortly after coming to Christ, one young person lost a close family member who was a major pillar in his life—and with the pillar gone, everything else became insecure. I also don't think we prepared young people for this sort of thing. Our emphasis was that Jesus could transform their lives, which is true, but this does not mean a trouble-free life. We should have balanced the truth about transformation with the truth about tribulation. Jesus warned his disciples, 'In the world ye shall have tribulation.' In other words, the Christian life is going to be tough. Yes, Christ will bring love, joy and freedom, but you may have to face some of the toughest circumstances in your life.

The relationship between faith and trials is an important issue to raise at this point. One of the main reasons I have for writing this book is that I want people to know that Jesus Christ can and does change lives. However, the gospel is not a happy pill. You will at some point 'walk through the valley of the shadow of death,' but the good news is that with Christ, you may 'fear no evil' because the one who holds the universe together is holding you together.

PRAGUE

One of the great things about being a student is the end of term. There were no classes from July to October. It was during these months that students would often get involved in mission, or they would organise residential and other summer activities. Paisley YMCA was off to Prague! Four leaders, including myself and David ,and about fourteen young people, a number of them from Feegie, went off to a European YMCA festival. It was a great opportunity for both the staff and young people. There were many highlights (and low points) during this trip, but a few of them in particular stick in my mind. As we travelled by tram through the emerging city of culture and civilisation, the Feegie boys, donning old-firm tops and trackie bottoms, couldn't seem to resist shouting out the window at passersby while giving them the universal sign of two fingers. (Isn't it amazing how young people from disadvantaged backgrounds can overcome cultural and linguistic barriers and find meaningful ways to communicate?) The whole scenario was like a scene from the TV show *Chewin' the Fat*. It was from instances like this that we coined the phrase, 'Fegs on Tour'. Of course, not everyone was from Feegie, but it seemed to sum up the antics quite well.

Like an episode of *EastEnders*, each day was a mixture of mundane activities and mini-dramas. The YMCA had booked university hostels on the outskirts of the city for the several thousand conference delegates who had come from all over the world. The hostels were large, dilapidated, stone block buildings clustered together in the middle of a wasteland. The only other premises were a dirty-looking pub, with tables outside and customers who were smoking cannabis, a dingy night club and a corner shop. Of course, some of our young people, along with some fellow youngsters from Glasgow, found their way to these premises straightaway.

Our accommodation had a reception desk which was manned by a local guy, probably a student, who didn't speak a word of English. Consequently, getting help with anything was all but impossible. Each of the rooms came with a safety deposit box and key. One of the guys had locked away his passport, wallet and money in the safety deposit box but had lost his key. After several failed attempts to explain his problem to the guy at reception, he returned to his room with one of his mates and did what any good Feegie lad in his situation would do. He broke into the safety deposit box.

When we met together for a team meeting, we were informed about what had taken place. David was leading the meeting, and he brought up the issue of the safety deposit box. The guy involved looked a bit sheepish; he was expecting a lecture. Instead, with the rhetorical excellence of a military commander, David turned the whole situation into a mock learning experience. 'Look all around you,' he said. 'Look at all these young people from all over the globe. Many of these young people come from successful backgrounds, they are well educated and they would perhaps look down upon young people from Ferguslie Park. But what would they do if they were in your situation? A lost key? No passport, no money, a locked safety deposit box and no way of communicating to the only member of staff. They would be stumped. They would go without money. But not you. You are Fegs. This day you have shown initiative by putting your breaking-and-entering skills to good use. You have shown the world that you will rise above the challenges that you face. Today is not a day to be ashamed of your environment; today is a day where you should be proud to be a Feg.'

David's banter set a good tone for the day. There had been some friction among the team, but by the end of his William Wallace-type speech, everyone was relaxed, full of laughter and proud to be a 'Feg'. While the trip to Prague had many challenges (which generally related to drunk young people, drunk staff members from other YMCAs, and drunk guys in their thirties from the Glasgow YMCA homeless accommodation), overall, the trip was a good experience for our young people. For a number of them, it was not just their first time abroad, but it was their first time out of Scotland.

There was a really dangerous incident at the end of the trip, though. The guys from the Glasgow YMCA homeless accommodation had spent the final night drinking outside the hostel. Some local guys were walking past when one of the Glasgow guys decided to shout abuse at him. One of the local guys ran towards him, pulled out a knife and stabbed him. A fight broke out, and there was a lot of shouting. Fortunately, David was quite experienced in these situations, and he was able to get right into the situation, break up the fight and help get the guy to hospital.

When I returned from Prague, I renewed my contract with YMCA and agreed to work with them for another twelve months. I also signed up for a second year of youth work studies. However, in my heart, I wanted to be studying a course which was more scripture based and gospel focused.

A Broader Ministry

This chapter is already almost twice the length of some other chapters in this book. If I were to write about everything that took place at the YM, it would soon become a book in its own right (and at least twice the length of this one). Paisley YMCA was a major preparation ground for me. However, as much as I loved working for the YM, there was always a sense that God's call on my life was broader than youth work and broader than the YMCA. It is to this broader calling that we now turn.

9

Training for Ministry

THE theological college where I studied was in Glasgow city centre. A few months into the course, I gave up my flat in Kilbarchan and moved into their student accommodation. Commuting from Glasgow to Paisley YMCA was much easier than commuting from Kilbarchan to Glasgow. Halfway through my second year, I moved back to Paisley. On returning there I reconnected with the leadership of the church at Beith. They were a husband-and-wife team, and they were in the process of converting an old garage into a new church facility. The church was a small, independent, Charismatic church with a huge vision for outreach and growth. In comparison with the secular emphasis of the YMCA, and the liberal emphasis of the theological college, it was like a pool of water in a dry wasteland. Here, the emphasis was not on analysing and questioning the Bible, but on believing and obeying the Bible. Of course, there is always a danger that a simple approach becomes a simplistic approach, but at this time in my walk with God, I needed to be around people who wanted to take the Bible seriously.

GRACE CHURCH

The church in Beith was going through a transition. Not only was it moving to other premises, it was changing its name to Grace Church Scotland, and it had embraced the cell-church vision which was designed to help equip the church for local mission. The cell-church vision is an approach which seeks to empower the larger church in its local areas to meet as small groups. Each church is made up of several small cell-groups; as each cell-group meets in its local area, that cell-group becomes a centre of evangelistic activity. As each group reaches out, the church begins to grow. The cells would meet weekly and then come together on the Sunday, to the main church centre, for a celebration service.

Looking back, I now understand that there were weaknesses in this approach to church, but that aside, I can honestly say that it is probably one of the most evangelistically focused churches I have ever been in.

Upon joining the church, the leaders asked me to join their leadership team and to consider planting a cell-group in Paisley. It was God's timing; the cell-group in Paisley took off. We were praying for people who did not know Christ to be saved, then inviting them to a small-group meeting which had a gospel focus. Consequently, there were a number of people who made professions of faith. One profession of faith in particular is worth mentioning.

I was in Paisley town centre when I bumped into Paddy, a young guy in his early twenties who used to volunteer at Paisley YMCA. Paddy was from a Catholic background, and during the season when a number of young people were turning to Christ, he had expressed an interest in the things of God. However, his interest did not last, and before long he stopped coming to the YMCA altogether. In the cell-groups, it was a common practice to pray for at least three people we were in contact with, so I decided to add Paddy's name to the list. We'd been praying for him for some time, and we had an outreach planned, so I decided to give him a call to see if he wanted to come to the meeting. When he answered the phone, he sounded down, and he declined the invite to the house group. However, my phone rang about five minutes later. It was Paddy, and he'd changed his mind and now wanted to come.

There were a number of unbelievers at the meeting; there were some visitors from another church as well as members of the cell-group. The night was made up of a short talk from one of the guys from the church, a video testimony, and an invitation to receive Christ as saviour and Lord. During the invitation, Paddy raised his hand to indicate that he wanted to receive Christ.

We went through to a spare room where I explained the gospel more fully to him, and especially focused on the need for repentance. He told me he had been visiting spiritualists because his girlfriend had suffered a miscarriage. I explained to him that spiritualism was incompatible with Christ and asked him if he still wanted to come to Christ if it meant he had to turn from spiritualism. He agreed. As he repented of his sins, using his own words, and called upon Christ for forgiveness and new life, he broke down in a flood of tears. He then began to cry out about how clean he felt. 'Why didn't I turn to Christ years ago?' he wept.

The whole encounter was very powerful. It was even more powerful when he returned to the main room and shared what had been happening in his life before he came to the meeting. Paddy told us that he'd been struggling with depression and that he was just about to end his own life. On the brink of suicide he cried out in desperation, 'God, please help me,' and just as he was about to take his life, the phone rang. It was me, inviting him to the meeting. He explained that after he'd said no and hung up the phone, he'd realised that this was his life-line: it was God answering his prayer.

SCOTTISH BAPTIST COLLEGE

By the time I'd completed the second year of the youth work course, I had a strong sense that I needed to broaden my area of study. I knew that I wasn't going to be in youth work until I retired. I decided to visit Paisley University to see if I could transfer my university credits over to one of their courses. As I was in the campus, I suddenly remembered that the Scottish Baptist College was situated in the Paisley campus, so I made my way there to make enquiries.

What happened next was a bit of a whirlwind. It was as if I knocked at the door and it opened and a gale carried me onto the course. It just so happened that I'd turned up on the very day the course had started. I was interviewed and told to start the next day. The college offered a four-year Bachelor of Divinity with Honours, and with the credits from my previous course, I was able to go straight into third year.

By this stage in my studies, I'd grown to really enjoy the process of learning. I think it took me until the end of second year before I stopped simply seeing study as a means to an end and actually started to enjoy the benefits of learning. Having said that, I still had contempt for academic pretentiousness, and the lack of fire and evangelistic fervour in the academic elites frustrated me no end.

On one occasion, it was my turn to preach at morning chapel. The text I had been given was from the Book of Acts. It was the passage of scripture which followed the healing of the man at the temple. It was about the evangelistic preaching that followed the demonstration of God's power. At this point in my walk with God, the Lord had been convicting me about getting back to simple evangelism. Prior to Bible college, I'd witnessed to people in a natural way, at bus stops, train stations and in the streets, anywhere there was an opportunity. However, having spent a few years at Bible college, it all seemed to be about academia and professionalism. As I was sharing these thoughts, in light of the passage from Acts, I found myself saying, 'Some of you have more letters after your name than there are in the alphabet—Rev, Dr, MTh, BD, www dot com—but when was the last time you led a soul to Christ?' I thought it was a great point; so did the students. Needless to say, I was surprised when I was called into the principal's office for a talking to. (With hindsight, I perhaps could have packaged that point a little more sensitively!)

The time at the Baptist College and the preaching engagements which were a part of the course soon paved the way for preaching engagements within local Baptist churches. At this point in my walk, I still wasn't a confident preacher. The idea of preparing sermons and using notes seemed suffocating to me. I preferred to share testimony and to preach 'off the cuff'. On one occasion, in a local Baptist church, I shared my testimony, preached the gospel and shared a word of encouragement. At the end of the service I got talking to a young guy who had visited the church. He was from one of the schemes in Paisley. He wasn't a Christian, and within several minutes he opened up about the level of crime and violence he had been involved in.

'Can God forgive anything?' he asked, his eyes boring into mine.

'Yes,' I said confidently.

'Even murder?'

I felt sick in my stomach. I got the impression that he wasn't just asking this question for hypothetical reasons.

'Yes, Moses was a murderer, and so was David, and so were many other people who have been saved and called by God.' I then proceeded to explain about the power of the cross and the need for all people to be saved.

However, as we were leaving the church, I sensed the Lord impress upon me to go and speak to him again. While he had not actually confessed to anything, I felt he had implied it. I also felt it was important to let him know that in order to know the freedom and salvation which is in Christ, he would need to be prepared to bring everything into the light, no matter the consequences.

DIVINE INTERVENTION

In January 2007, a few months before the course was drawing to a close, I began to consider what I would do next. Perth Baptist Church was advertising for a youth pastor so I decided to apply for it. I visited the church. It was a very affluent church, but the people seemed to have a genuine heart to reach the community. I applied for the post, went for a few interviews and was offered the job in April with a view to start in August. I loved the city of Perth; it was like the country and the city rolled into one.

I finished my studies in May, and I wasn't moving to Perth until August, so for the next few months I helped a local pastor with a church he was planting in another area. After a few months of supporting the meetings and helping with outreach, the time for heading to Perth was drawing near. In the few months that I'd been involved with the church plant, I'd also connected with a number of the church members via social network. One of the members I'd connected with was Laura, the praise and worship leader. Laura and I had not really spoken much, but we interacted a little on social network and as a result, ended up organising a night out for the youth. I also asked her if she wanted to meet up for coffee; it just so happened that the only time we could manage coffee was the day after we were taking the youth to the cinema.

As we were at the cinema, we noticed that the latest *Die Hard* movie was also on, and after we dropped the young people off at their homes, we decided to go back to the cinema for a late viewing. As Laura dropped me off at my flat, we started chatting, sharing our testimonies and talking about life and the things of the Lord. Seven hours passed. (I always say, I have no idea where the time went, but I know that Laura did more talking than me!) It was about six in the morning, and we were supposed to be meeting up in four hours!

We met at ten o'clock as arranged, but we never made it for the coffee; instead, we walked up a hill, flew a kite, strolled along Irvine Beach, sat chatting and looking out to sea and realised that we hadn't eaten a thing. We headed to Largs for a mixed Pakora takeway. It was just a very chilled, carefree and enjoyable day.

As we were chatting during the drive home, we were talking about our plans for the future and what we both believed God was calling us to as individuals. Both of us were at a major junction in our lives. We both had fixed plans in place. I was about to move to Perth, and she was in the process of selling her house and was planning to do some world travel. However, God had other plans.

10

New Directions

THE day after I met up with Laura, there was a visiting preacher at church, and he was preaching about the plan and purpose of God: 'For we are God's handiwork, created in Christ Jesus to do good works, which God prepared in advance for us to do' (Ephesians 2:10). For some reason, I sensed the Lord convicting me through the message. The preacher kept emphasising that 'God *had* a plan and purpose for you.' These things are always subjective, but within myself I felt the Lord challenging me on the direction I was taking.

I spent the remainder of the day and evening in prayer. As I did so, there was a strong sense that I was not to take the job in Perth and that God still had a purpose for me in Paisley. The scriptures and the sense of the Holy Spirit's leading impacted me so strongly that I couldn't ignore it. However, I had a problem—I was about to move house and start a new job in Perth in the next few weeks! After much prayer and soul searching, I came to the conclusion that I needed to turn down the job in Perth.

After following through with my sense of conviction that the Lord had plans for me in Paisley, almost immediately the Lord propelled me in a completely new direction. Through a number of unusual circumstances, in both Laura's life and my own, we found ourselves sensing that our meeting had not been coincidental. In fact, the Lord's sovereign hand had brought us together. Laura and I were dating by August, engaged in the autumn, and married before Christmas. The Lord soon blessed us both with two amazing sons, Ethan John and Caleb Joel.

BACK TO SCHOOL
With our first child on the way and the lack of security which accompanies short-term youth work contracts, I decided to apply for teacher training in Religious Education. There was an obstacle, however; the entry requirements were a degree in a relevant subject *and* Higher English. As I said earlier, I didn't have a Higher to my name; the only way I got into university was because of my experience in the field of youth work. However, upon making enquiries, the guy who ran the course informed me that on some occasions, they are willing to receive a few examples of the applicant's written work, and if it is considered to be an adequate standard, a place could still be offered. The door opened.

Being back in a school environment was not comfortable at first. As I made my way through the corridors and into staff rooms, I felt my mouth turning dry and my palms beginning to sweat. I felt out of my depth. Yet the years of youth work experience carried me through the placements and the course. The Lord empowered me to develop skills in teaching and to design lessons in a way that helped young people engage with the subject.

Having gone from posts in informal youth work and drug crisis projects to teaching has created both challenges and opportunities for sharing the message of Jesus Christ. The RE classroom is not a church, and the role of the RE teacher is to help young people explore their own worldview. Likewise with colleagues, there is not the same freedom to speak about Christ that there is perhaps in a building site or in a factory. In a world of professional attitudes and political values, you need to weave your way through very sensitively. However, the Lord has opened doors of opportunity in various places.

As my teacher training studies were drawing to a close and my probationary period was about to start, I received an unexpected letter from the General Teaching Council of Scotland (GTCS); they were making enquiries about a few charges which had shown up on my disclosure form. These covered a couple of breaches of the peace and a few vandalism charges. What was ironic was the fact that the letter basically stated that GTCS were sure that there had been some sort of mix-up and all I had to do was confirm that these charges were in fact not mine. Well, that would be hard to do! I wrote back, explaining the circumstances at the time, telling them how I had heard the gospel and how it had changed my life. In particular, I emphasised that for the last eight years, I had been working with young people who were engaged in the same 'at risk' behaviours through projects that were set up to help them. I then concluded with the statement that I hoped that my background, along with the charges, rather than being an indication of my unsuitability for teaching, would actually be an advantage! I drew attention to the fact that Scotland has many schools in urban deprivation areas, and that education is about empowerment. In other words, education is a tool to help people overcome the social barriers which keep them locked in a life of poverty.

I'm not sure if the GTCS had ever received a letter like mine. However, I sent it with the confidence that God had led me into teaching; He hadn't done so in order that I would deny my background or His saving grace.

One of my final pieces of work for teacher training was a research project and presentation for the Citizenship module. I explored how the media portray young people, how adults perceive young people and how young people feel that they are perceived. As one aspect of this, I explored the media's obsession with youth gang cultures and how their portrayal of youth culture causes society to assume that all young people are thugs.

One of the lecturers was really impressed with my presentation, and he invited me to attend a conference at the university which was focused on the destructive behaviours of young people from urban priority areas. (It was basically a conference highlighting the problems which young people face in the schemes and exploring ways to help combat the problem.) I was encouraged by the fact that the lecturer had invited me. I agreed to go to the conference.

The conference was attended by a multitude of agencies: social work, police, teachers and many others. There were a number of presentations along with some videos which showed the seriousness of Scotland's problems associated with juvenile delinquency. As the final talk was coming to an end, I felt my phone vibrate in my pocket. It was a text message. I took a sneaky wee glance at my phone; it was Laura: 'GTCS letter arrived today. I thought you'd want to know their decision ASAP. So I opened it; it says they disapprove of the behaviour associated with the charges but have agreed, in light of the information and evidence you have supplied, to grant you full registration.' This was a major relief; I really wasn't sure what decision the GTCS were going to arrive at. My attention returned to the presentation. The final speaker was drawing attention to the lack of solutions to gang culture problems. A thought struck me. Here I was sitting in this meeting which was all about 'at risk' young people and youth crime. And here am I, having just received confirmation from the GTCS that they will allow me to become a teacher despite my own involvement with youth crime. Here were all these agencies looking for answers to the problem, and here was I, someone who had found the answer in Jesus Christ. At this point the person who was chairing the meeting asked if anyone would like to contribute anything. My heart began to race. I knew I needed to share this. A few agencies chipped in, but there was a real sense of hopelessness. No one had any real answers. I raised my hand.

'Hi, everyone, I'm John, and I have just completed my teacher training. But before I start, a few minutes ago I received a text message, and I had a sneaky peek while the last speaker was still talking.' The room rippled with laughter. 'As I sit here today, I can identify with many of the videos shown and the information we received. As a teenager, I grew up in schemes just like the ones we have seen today. I engaged in many of the behaviours which we have seen today. The text message I received a few moments ago was from my wife, confirming that the GTCS have decided to allow me into teaching even though I have a criminal record—a record which serves as a reminder of my behaviour as a teenager. I understand today that many of us are looking for answers to the problems associated with youth crime. Let me tell you how I found the answer. As a teenager I stumbled upon a local church, and I heard the gospel of Jesus Christ. As I believed the gospel, my life was turned completely around. I would encourage all the agencies represented here today, as you seek to respond to the problems related to gang cultures, to please consider partnering with local churches. There are many local churches all over Scotland which are doing great work with some of the most broken and vulnerable people in our society.'

At the end of the conference, the lecturer who had invited me approached me and thanked me for not only attending but for my input and what I had said about local churches. He ended up sharing with me that he was a Christian and an elder in a local Church of Scotland. As I reflected on the situation, I appreciated afresh the importance of Christians being in every sphere of society, but I was also aware of the importance of the need for Christians to have a voice. Society is broken and looking for answers, the church is the only true hope for the nation and we need to demonstrate the power of the gospel within the communities where God has placed us.

The Highlands

After completing my probationary period at Inverclyde Academy, a job came up in the Highlands. Both Laura and I felt this was the Lord's leading. The door opened, and we relocated to the Highlands in July 2010. This part of Scotland has some of the most stunning scenery on the face of the earth. A few years after we moved here, I was thinking about the differences between life in the scheme and life in the Highlands. The following poem was a result of my thoughts.

'Scotland's Scenes'
Miles of misty, mysterious hills,
The heart enlarges, the mind is stilled,

Scenic Scotland, the soul it thrills,
Its haunting landscape excites and chills.
Vast beaches, barren, blazing white sand,
Towering cliffs, so majestic and grand,
Forever on your soul, their image, they brand,
It is not difficult to understand,
Why many are drawn to Bonnie Scotland.
A peninsular postcard: picturesque,
A coastal cliff coaster, for your desk.
Spectacular scenes, a mountainous view,
But is this the only Scotland you knew?
Eclipsed by splendid, saintly scenes,
Lie Scotland's dark and hellish schemes,
Concrete jungles, an urban zoo,
This is the Scotland you never knew.
Tower blocks and run-down tenement flats,
Next-door neighbours, just nameless stats.
Community crumbling, individual's reign,
'Survival of the fittest' is the name of the game.
While drug-dealers claim 'The American Dream',
Poverty, pain, powerlessness, mark the scheme,
Addiction, hopelessness, crime: the theme,
'Bonnie Scotland' aint so Bonnie it would seem.
Fatherless families fight through their fears,
Young people drowning in drugs and beers,
Pop pills, numb the pain, and resist the tears,
A silent cry, which no one hears.
Emptiness: the inheritance, of this generation,
A hollow shell, this soulless nation.
A barren land; a waterless brook,
An empty Kirk; a forgotten book.
Be gone with your romantic Scottish vision!
The land lies dying, in need of mission.

When I wrote this poem, I was thinking about the romantic view of Scotland that many tourists have. It is easy to visit Scotland from across the world and assume that the peaceful, picturesque lochs and coastlines are the whole story. However, there is an important aspect of Highland life that my poem does not highlight; it neglects to mention the fact that the Highlands are no Garden of Eden. Human brokenness may not be so explicitly evident in rural areas, but it exists nonetheless. A pastor of a church in the Highlands once said:

> Hidden from view in these highland glens are the manic depressive and the alcoholic, families torn in two, and a new generation with no reason to expect anything from the church. Human need is not confined to urban housing schemes. As a Christian living in a scenic paradise, I have to regularly remind myself that this is why I am here.

His point is powerful. It is not just the schemes that are in need of redemption; the country is also deeply in need of God's transforming grace, with the gospel being taken to both the country and the city.

However, there is another point which needs to be made. While the gospel produces social transformation, this itself is not the heart of the gospel; it is simply the effect of the gospel. The gospel has the power to restore alcoholics, drug addicts and manic depressives, but its primary concern is to restore our relationship with God. The gospel is designed to reconcile us, redeem us and make us righteous.

FINAL THOUGHTS

This chapter is called New Directions, but in many ways the whole book is all about finding new direction. Perhaps you are reading this book and your life is also in need of a new direction. Perhaps you have taken a wrong turn, and as a result you are wandering through life aimless and lost. Maybe you are reading this although you cannot personally identify with the social chaos described in the pages. Whatever your situation, I hope this book has demonstrated that the gospel is relevant for you.

The Bible is clear that all people who live on the earth have wandered from God: 'All we like sheep have gone astray; we have turned—every one—to his own way;' (Isaiah 53:6). We have all sinned and rejected God. Consequently, we are lost and without hope, and there is nothing we can do to change this. God himself is the only one who can change this situation. The word 'gospel' means 'good news'. The good news is that God has given his Son Jesus Christ as a substitute. He died in our place, and he received God's righteous anger instead of us. The brutality of the cross is an expression of God's mercy and judgement. Christ is judged for sins that were not His so that we might receive mercy and a righteousness that is not ours. Jesus is righteous, and we are the rebels: 'The Lord has laid on him the iniquity of us all.' (Isaiah 53:6).

Ultimately, there are two directions that every human being may take. There is a road which leads to hell and a road which leads to heaven. Christ alone is the road to heaven. If this book has impacted you in any way, I urge you to turn to Christ, turn from your sin, and receive his free gift of eternal life.

I have written this book for a wide variety of readers. I hope that it is helpful to young people who are caught in a web of destructive behaviours. I hope people who are bound in addictions find help within its pages. I hope that Christians who read it are inspired by the goodness and power of God. I hope that unbelievers, who from a social point of view seem to have it 'all together', will also find that the message of this book leads them to think about their own need of Christ. Above all, I hope that God uses this book for His own purpose and His glory and that many who read it will be drawn to the saviour.

> *Amazing grace! How sweet the sound*
> *That saved a wretch like me!*
> *I once was lost, but now am found;*
> *Was blind, but now I see.*

About the Author

John Caldwell lives on the Isle of Skye with his wife, Laura, and two sons, Ethan and Caleb. John serves as Ministry Assistant for Bracadale and Portree Free Church of Scotland congregations and is also a school teacher.